Contents

Chapter 1: Defining the Model in GORM

The Goal of GORM

When you stop for a moment to consider what we are doing, it is really astounding. We are trying to comprehend some kind of process or system with all of its emergent and dynamic aspects, with its historical artifacts and experimental features, and to somehow encode that comprehension onto an electrically-charged platter. Most of the time, we're not just adjusting the electrical charge on the platter in front of us, though—that'd be too easy. We want to encode the information of this system into some electrically-charged platter that we have never even seen, and have only experienced by way of many, many levels of intermediaries. In short, we are communicating the behavior of an entire system to an electrically charged platter far away via an astoundingly automated game of telephone.

There seems to be two approaches when it comes time to accomplish this daunting, seemingly magical feat: the first approach begins with deep analysis of the application's domain, involves conversations where the breadth of the domain is identified and the intricacies of the relationships are explored, and finally creates the model in code (the analyst's approach); the second creates class definitions as they become relevant to functionality and relies on dynamic restructuring to handle new developments (the hacker's approach). In either case, certain qualities of GORM (Grails Object Relational Mapping) make it a very advantageous ORM technology.

For the hacker, GORM consolidates the current class definition into a single, quickly written, easily read file. That single file defines the class's properties, functionality, and relationships, which means changes to the class definition are always reflected in a single place.

For the analyst, GORM provides a very rich set of configuration options with many convenient default settings, while also letting you adjust the configuration to best fit within the envisioned system.

For either hacker or analyst, working with GORM starts the same way—by defining the model objects.

Defining Objects in GORM

Fundamentally, a GORM domain class is simply a Groovy class placed under `./grails-app/domain`. By its location, Grails infers that it is a GORM domain class and attaches to it a full set of default metadata and functionality. This metadata provides a default set of mappings from Groovy objects onto the database. These mappings are usually sufficient for development purposes and small applications. However, when the time does come for some custom configuration, metadata configuration of the GORM domain class is done by defining static properties on the class.

Creating and Defining Simple Domain Classes

To generate a simple domain class with the name "Foo," execute `grails create-domain-class Foo` in the root of your Grails application. This creates two files in your application: `./grails-app/domain/Foo.groovy` and `./test/integration/FooTests.groovy`. The first file defines the domain class, and the second provides a place to write tests for that class.

Caution   When naming your classes and properties, watch out for SQL and Hibernate Query Language keywords. These keywords will cause problems when Grails tries to map your object onto the database. Should you run into this problem, the simplest solution is to customize the offending name. See the "Custom Names" section later in this chapter for more on this.

Opening up `./grails-app/domain/Foo.groovy`, we find it very barren.

Code Listing 1-1. The Foo Domain Class at Generation

```
// In ./grails-app/domain/Foo.groovy
class Foo {
}
```

Despite the emptiness of the class, quite a bit has already gone on: when the Grails application is run, this class will ensure the database matches up with the class definition and inject an entire site of querying functionality onto the class, as well as other functionality such as optimistic locking. There is a lot here, so let's open up the test file at `./test/integration/FooTests.groovy` to exercise the basics. As it sits, that file is frightfully empty.

Code Listing 1-2. The Foo Domain Class Tests at Generation

```
// In ./test/integration/FooTests.groovy
class FooTests extends GroovyTestCase {
  void testSomething() {
  }
}
```

Tip   Facing down an empty test class can cause coder's block in even the most experienced developers. To get over this hurdle I always write my first test as simply `assertTrue(true)`, and then execute that to verify my testing framework is set up correctly. The next test seems a lot easier to write once there's already something on the page. This test will also catch any exceptions in the testing framework or test class setup and teardown.

Let's begin by exercising some of the functionality that Grails provides for free.

Code Listing 1-3. Demonstrating the `id` Property

```
// In ./test/integration/FooTests.groovy
void testId() {
  def foo = new Foo()
  assertNull     foo.id
  assertNotNull foo.save() // Asserts no errors
  assertNotNull foo.id      // Set in save
  assertEquals  Long, foo.id.class
}
```

Although we did not declare an `id` property, Grails has provided one for us. The property is the artificial identifier and primary key for the database row, so it is not set until the record is saved into the database with `.save()`.

Another property that Grails provides is the `version` property, which it uses to manage optimistic locking. To exercise the `version` property, though, we first need to provide a new property to change.

Code Listing 1-4. Adding the `bar` Property

```
// In ./grails-app/domain/Foo.groovy
class Foo {
  int bar
}
```

Simply declaring the property is all that it takes: Grails handles the database migration and provides reasonable default property metadata for you. In order to do this, the property must be statically typed, and of a type recognizable to Hibernate—all the primitive types (including String) are.

Now that we have a property on our domain class we can exercise the `version` property.

Code Listing 1-5. Demonstrating the version Property

```groovy
// In ./test/integration/FooTests.groovy
void testVersion() {
  def foo = new Foo()
  assertNotNull foo.save()
  def version = foo.version
  foo.bar++
  assertNotNull foo.save(flush:true)
  assertEquals version+1, foo.version
}
```

The `version` property increments after each save to the database, which is how GORM implements optimistic locking. Optimistic locking is provided for free: you do not have to do anything with the `version` property except stay out of its way. You can find details on using optimistic locking in Chapter 4.

Note   There is some caching going on in Code Listing 2-5. If you remove `flush:true` from the second `save` call, the test will fail. This is because calls to `save()` do not normally hit the database until the end of the transaction, but we force the save and the associated version increment by calling `save(flush:true)`.

Grails does not just provide properties and background functionality, though, it also provides an entire set of static data access methods. For more information on these, see Chapter 3.

Creating and Defining Inheritance Trees

One of the most major breaks between the relational and object-oriented paradigm is the concept of inheritance: while relational databases handle *has-a* relationships just fine via foreign keys, they do not have a clear way to mirror *is-a* relationships. This has been a pain point in many ORM technologies where an object-oriented programmer wants to define a model where behavior is inherited, but has to somehow hack a *has-a* relationship in the metadata to line things up in the database.

In Grails, extending a class is straightforward and works exactly how you would guess it would. Let's begin by executing `grails create-domain-class Product` and `grails create-domain-class Book` to create two domain classes. We will make `Book` extend `Product` through standard Java inheritance.

Code Listing 1-6. Product and Book Class Definitions

```
// In ./grails-app/domain/Product.groovy
class Product {
  String name
}


// In ./grails-app/domain/Book.groovy
class Book extends Product {
  String author
}
```

The `name` and `author` properties exist solely to demonstrate the polymorphic nature of `Book` and `Product`. These could be empty classes if you so desired. Beyond telling `Book` to extend `Product`, there is literally no further configuration needed to handle this polymorphic relationship—a polymorphic relationship is now stored in the database and reflected throughout GORM.

Code Listing 1-7. Demonstrating Domain Class Polymorphism

```groovy
// In ./test/integration/BookTests.groovy
void testBookIsProduct() {
  assertEquals 0, Product.list().size()
  def book = new Book(name: 'Book', author: 'Author')
  assertNotNull book.save()
  assertNotNull Product.get(book.id)
  assertEquals book.name, Product.get(book.id).name
  assertEquals book.author, Product.get(book.id).author
  assertEquals Book, Product.get(book.id).class
}
```

As the test in the previous code listing shows, you can save a Book object and then retrieve it using the Product structure: the Book *is-a* Product, so queries on Product reflect the newly existing Book. Even more, the Product query is smart enough to return a Book class, so you have direct access to the author property.

In the background Grails is creating only a single table—product—which contains the attributes for both the Product and Book domain classes. In addition to the standard automatic properties (id, version), there is also a class column that specifies the class the row represents. Do not try to work with the class column directly: as the last assert in the previous code listing demonstrates, it is not accessible as a GORM property (it is hidden by the Object method getClass()) and simply acts as metadata.

Although this approach performs very well and behaves in intuitive ways, the single-table-per-tree approach to inheritance has a few nuances that a developer needs to be aware of. The most obvious nuance is the somewhat incongruous definition of the author column on the product table: whereas GORM defaults to defining all columns as not null, the author column is defined as nullable in the database. Despite that column definition, the `author` field cannot be set to `null`, as the next code listing proves.

Code Listing 1-8. Demonstrating How Child Class Properties Enforce the Nullability Constraint

```
// In ./test/integration/BookTests.groovy
void testAuthorIsNotNullable() {
  def book = new Book(name: 'Book', author: 'Author')
  assertNotNull book.save()
  book.author = null
  assertNull book.save()
  assertNull book.errors.getFieldError('name')
  assertNotNull book.errors.getFieldError('author')
}
```

As long as the table is accessed via this GORM method, there is no concern about data integrity here. However, some people will be uncomfortable having a nullable column in a table that should not be able to hold the null value in the model's property.

Astute readers are already identifying a tricky problem: what about two classes in the same tree that have the same property name but different data types? GORM handles this transparently. It reuses the column but uses the more general data type. For instance, given our `Book` with a `String` `author` property, let's see what happens when we define a `Book2` with an `int` `author` property.

Code Listing 1-9. Definition of `Book2` with a Conflicting Property Type

```
// In ./grails-app/domain/Book2.groovy
class Book2 extends Product {
  int author
}
```

When this class is executed the database is left with the data type corresponding to String, but integer values are inserted into it. Both the String author and int author properties still work, and GORM ensures that the developer will never notice the difference, as Code Listing 1-10 demonstrates.

Code Listing 1-10. Demonstrating Coexisting Conflicting Columns

```
// In ./test/integration/Book2Tests.groovy
void testCanAddIntAuthor() {
  def book = new Book(name:'Book', author:'Author')
  def book2 = new Book2(name:'Book2', author:2)
  assertNotNull book.save()
  assertNotNull book2.save()
  assertEquals String, Book.get(book.id).author.class
  assertEquals Integer, Book2.get(book2.id).author.class
}
```

Another nuance is that every attribute for every class in the tree is in the single parent table. This means that if you have a very deep tree or a significant number of properties on child classes, you can end up with a very broad table, most of which is unused for certain classes. This is generally not a noticeable impact on performance or storage size, but it does encourage small classes and shallow inheritance trees.

If you run into a situation where you can prove that the unused columns or conflicting datatypes are a significant issue, GORM does give you another way to define inheritance trees: instead of storing all the subclasses into one very large table you can give each subclass its own table to store additional information. This eliminates any issue around unused and conflicting columns, but at the expense of creating additional tables in the database and requiring many expensive joins at fetch time. As a general rule, this alternative approach is not preferable to the single-table approach because of performance issues and behavior inconsistencies, but Grails gives you the option to do it if you really insist. For more information on this approach, see the "Mapping Inheritance" section later in this chapter.

Adding Functionality to One Domain Class

Once you have your class defined you simply have a wrapper around the relational tables that exist in the database, perhaps with a bit of polymorphism for good measure. That model is not really object-oriented, though, until those classes get behaviors.

Custom Methods and Artificial Properties

Methods are the backbone of object-oriented programming in Groovy, and they are the defined in GORM domain classes just as they are defined for any other Groovy object. As with any other Groovy object, methods in a domain class may have either implicit or explicit return values.

Code Listing 1-11. Defining User Methods on a Domain Class

```
// In ./grails-app/domain/Foo.groovy
class Foo {
  int bar
  def returnTrue() { return !returnFalse() }
  boolean returnFalse() { return false }
}
```

Code Listing 1-12. Testing User Methods on a Domain Class

```
// In ./test/integration/FooTests.groovy
void testLogHelloAndLogGoodbyeReturnValues() {
  def foo = new Foo()
  assertTrue foo.returnTrue()
  assertFalse foo.returnFalse()
}
```

In addition to standard behavior methods, GORM also gives the user the ability to define artificial properties. Artificial properties are not declared as normal properties, but instead are declared by providing a getter and/or a setter following a particular naming convention. By defining only getters or only setters you can create read-only or write-only properties that are accessible through the standard GPath dot notation, but that are not mapped into the database in any way. As an example, in Code Listing 1-13 the readOnly, writeOnly, and readWrite properties are not reflected in the database and are simply convenience methods for the user of the class.

Tip   A very common trick with artificial properties is using them to maintain backward compatibility with earlier versions of a class. If a property's data moves to a new name or even a different domain object, an artificial property can provide access under the old name and thereby maintain behavior. This can save you from having to update areas of code built off the previous version of the domain class.

Code Listing 1-13. Defining Artificial Properties

```groovy
// In ./grails-app/domain/Foo.groovy
def getReadOnly() { 'This is read only' }
def setWriteOnly(String toSet) {
  /* Ignored */
}
def getReadWrite() {
  System.getProperty('eg.read.write')
}
def setReadWrite(toSet) {
  System.setProperty('eg.read.write', toSet)
}
```

The methods in Code Listing 1-13 provide the Foo domain class with three artificial properties: readOnly, writeOnly, and readWrite. Since only a getter and no setter are provided for readOnly, the property is read only. Since only a setter and no getter is provided for writeOnly, that property is write only. And since we provided both a setter and a getter for readWrite, it is both readable and writable. This behavior is demonstrated in Code Listing 1-14. Note that due to the dynamic nature of the Groovy language, attempting to inappropriately access a read-only or write-only property is a runtime exception and not a compile-time error.

Code Listing 1-14. Demonstrating Artificial Properties

```
// In ./test/integration/FooTests.groovy
void testArtificialProperties() {
  def foo = new Foo()
  foo.writeOnly = 'This is write only!'
  shouldFail(MissingPropertyException) {
    foo.writeOnly
  }
  assertEquals 'This is read only', foo.readOnly
  shouldFail(ReadOnlyPropertyException) {
    // Slight asymmetry, but parent class is same
    assertTrue(ReadOnlyPropertyException instanceof
                      MissingPropertyException)
    foo.readOnly = 'Trying to save read only!'
  }
  assertEquals 'This is read only', foo.readOnly
  assertNull foo.readWrite
  foo.readWrite = 'Read and write'
  assertEquals 'Read and write', foo.readWrite
}
```

Default Property Values

Default values in GORM are defined in exactly the same way as the default values from any other Groovy object: simply follow the declaration with an assignment, as demonstrated in Code Listing 1-15.

Code Listing 1-15. Assigning a Default Property Value

```
// In ./grails-app/domain/Foo.groovy
class Foo {
  int bar = 42
}
```

This change provides a default value for the bar property. New instances of Foo will automatically have their bar set to 42. It's important to note that this value is assigned programmatically and is not reflected in the database schema itself. That is, while objects of this class are created with the value initialized appropriately, the database column backing the property will not generate database-provided default values.

Transient Properties

Often a domain class instance will track information that should not be stored in the database. The most common example is the cached value of an expensive calculation, or temporary data that is persisted by way of an event behavior (see the "Events" section). These unpersisted properties are called "transient", and transient properties are declared through the use of the transients static property. Many other Java-based ORM frameworks use the over-abused transient modifier keyword, but GORM goes a different route.

Code Listing 1-16. Declaring a `transient` Property

```
// In ./grails-app/domain/Foo.groovy
class Foo {
  static transients = ['frood', 'notStored']
  int bar
  String notStored
  String frood = "Ix"
}
```

Transient properties are not persisted to the database, but exist simply as fields on the object instance itself. Objects freshly fetched from the database will have the default value for those properties, no matter what previous value may have been set before a `save()` call. The one catch to this relates to caching. Instances of the class may be cached, in which case the transient properties are cached as well. This is normally to the user's advantage, but can be a bit surprising if the user is not ready for it. See Code Listing 1-17 for a demonstration.

Code Listing 1-17. Demonstrating Transient Properties and Caching

```
// In ./test/integration/FooTests.groovy
class FooTests extends GroovyTestCase {

  // Spring-injected handle on the
  // Hibernate SessionFactory
  def sessionFactory

  void testSessionFactoryIsNotNull() {
    assertNotNull sessionFactory
  }

  void testDemonstrateTransients() {
    def foo = new Foo()
```

```
        assertEquals "Ix", foo.frood
        foo.bar = 1
        assertNotNull foo.save()
        foo.frood = "Ford"
        foo.notStored = "Value"
        // Grab onto the foo instance id
        def fooId = foo.id

        // Demonstrate the caching of transient values
        foo = null
        foo = Foo.get(fooId)
        assertEquals 1, foo.bar
        assertEquals "Ford", foo.frood
        assertEquals "Value", foo.notStored

        // Clear session cache, clear the transient values
        foo = null
        sessionFactory.currentSession.clear()
        foo = Foo.get(fooId)
        assertNotNull foo
        assertEquals 1, foo.bar
        assertEquals "Ix", foo.frood
        assertNull foo.notStored
    }
```

Automatic Timestamping

Having domain objects track their creation and last update dates is a very
common requirement. So common, in fact, that GORM has a very simple
baked-in solution: the `dateCreated` and `lastUpdated` properties. Simply
adding these properties to the class triggers the automatic timestamping
functionality.

Code Listing 1-18. Defining Automatic Timestamping Properties

```groovy
// In ./grails-app/domain/Foo.groovy
class Foo {
  Date dateCreated, lastUpdated
  int bar
}
```

***Code Listing 1-19. Demonstrating Automatic Timestamping
Properties***

```groovy
// In ./test/integration/FooTests.groovy
void testAutomaticTimestamping() {
  def foo = new Foo()
  foo.bar = 1
  assertNull foo.dateCreated
  assertNull foo.lastUpdated
  assertNotNull foo.save()
  assertNotNull foo.dateCreated
  assertNotNull foo.lastUpdated
  def oldDateCreated = foo.dateCreated
  def oldLastUpdated = foo.lastUpdated
  foo.bar = 2
  assertNotNull foo.save()
  assertEquals oldDateCreated, foo.dateCreated
  assertEquals oldLastUpdated, foo.lastUpdated
  assertNotNull foo.save(flush:true)
  assertTrue foo.lastUpdated.after(oldLastUpdated)
}
```

Note that in Code Listing 1-19 we have the same kind of caching situation
we saw while working with the version property. Although the
lastUpdated and dateCreated properties are both initially set on the first
call to foo.save(), lastUpdated is not updated as part of the

`foo.save()` update calls; rather it is updated when the object is actually flushed to the database.

Caution   A naïve approach to optimistic locking is to use something like the `lastUpdated` timestamp to track update times on the erroneous interpretation of `lastUpdated` and `version` being somewhat redundant. Using `lastUpdated` in this way does not work due to data type issues: all timestamp types have a window of time where two different moments have the same timestamp value, and for some of the timestamp types this window can be as long as a few seconds. If you use such a value to implement an optimistic locking scheme, you end up creating the potential for a race condition, where two updates get the same timestamp value and hence circumvent the optimistic locking you thought you had. A common response is to say that the odds of this occurring in such a way as to cause a problem is very low, but due to the transactional nature of database work, this is also less true than one might think. With the cost of implementation for GORM's built-in optimistic locking being so low, it is almost certainly not worth the risk to use the naïve approach to locking using `lastUpdated`.

Events

Although event-driven logic waxes and wanes in popularity, its usefulness for tracking metadata such as `lastUpdated` and `dateCreated` is undeniable. Other popular uses include storing summary or audit data, calculating cached values up front, and logging. Event-driven logic hooks into the GORM objects through four properties: `beforeInsert`, `beforeUpdate`, `beforeDelete`, `onLoad`. These properties are assigned a closure that is executed at the corresponding time in an object's life cycle. The `beforeInsert` closure will be executed before the object is inserted into the database, the `beforeUpdate` closure will be executed before the database is updated with new data, the `beforeDelete` closure will be executed before the database record representing this object is deleted, and the `onLoad` closure will be executed when the object is first loaded from the database.

Code Listing 1-20. Example of Defining Events

```groovy
// In ./grails-app/domain/Foo.groovy
class Foo {
  int bar
  boolean beforeInsertFired = false
  boolean beforeUpdateFired = false
  boolean onLoadFired = false
  def beforeInsert = {
    beforeInsertFired = true
  }
  def beforeUpdate = {
    beforeUpdateFired = true
  }
  def beforeDelete = {
    // This code executed before a delete
  }
  def onLoad = {
    onLoadFired = true
  }
}
```

Understanding exactly when an event is going to fire is a bit tricky because the events are triggered by the actual persistence events. As we saw in the caching examples before, persistence events are often distinct from the calls that enqueue them.

Both `beforeInsert` and `beforeDelete` fire off when you would expect: `beforeInsert` fires off immediately at the execution of the `save` method on an instance that needs to go into the database, and `beforeDelete` fires off immediately at the execution of the `delete` method.

Code Listing 1-21. Demonstrating the `beforeInsert` Event

```
// In ./test/integration/FooTests.groovy
  void testEventFiringAtInsert() {
    def foo = new Foo()
    foo.bar = 1
    assertFalse foo.beforeInsertFired
    assertNotNull foo.save()
    assertTrue foo.beforeInsertFired
  }
```

In the following code listing, note that we assign the `beforeDelete` property externally. This is not to be construed as good practice as it overwrites any existing definition, but since setting a property on a class being deleted does not really make sense, we needed something for the sake of demonstration.

Code Listing 1-22. Demonstrating the `beforeDelete` Event

```
  void testEventFiringAtDelete() {
    def foo = new Foo()
    foo.bar = 1
    assertNotNull foo.save(flush:true)
    def fooId = foo.id
    boolean deleteFired = false
    foo.beforeDelete = { deleteFired = true }
    foo.delete()
    assertNull Foo.get(fooId)
    assertTrue deleteFired
  }
```

The `beforeUpdate` event does not fire immediately when `save` is called, but rather when the session is flushed to the database. Although this seems a bit surprising, the significant advantage is that multiple redundant firings of the `beforeUpdate` event are avoided in favor of a single firing at the very end of all the work. If you ever want to force the `beforeUpdate` event to fire you can either call it explicitly (e.g. `foo.beforeUpdate()`) or flush your save to the database immediately by saving with flush set to true (e.g. `foo.save(flush:true)`).

Code Listing 1-23. Demonstrating the `beforeUpdate` Event

```
void testEventFiringAtUpdate() {
   def foo = new Foo()
   foo.bar = 1
   assertNotNull foo.save()
   foo.beforeInsertFired = false
   foo.bar = 2
   assertNotNull foo.save()
   assertFalse foo.beforeInsertFired
   assertFalse foo.beforeUpdateFired
   sessionFactory.currentSession.flush()
   assertTrue foo.beforeUpdateFired
}
```

The `onLoad` event has an optimization similar to the `beforeUpdate` optimization: instead of firing whenever the object is retrieved by GORM, the event is only fired when a domain class instance is fetched from the database. If GORM retrieves the instance from the cache, the `onLoad` event does not fire. This is probably what you want to have happen in any case. After all, if GORM retrieved the instance from the cache, the work done by the `onLoad` event has already been applied to the retrieved object, and applying it again would be redundant.

Code Listing 1-24. Demonstrating the `onLoad` Event

```
// In ./test/integration/FooTests.groovy
  void testEventFiringAtLoad() {
    def foo = new Foo()
    foo.bar = 1
    assertNotNull foo.save()
    foo = Foo.get(foo.id)
    assertFalse foo.onLoadFired
    sessionFactory.currentSession.clear()
    foo = Foo.get(foo.id)
    assertTrue foo.onLoadFired
  }
```

Tip   There are a number of very good plugins in this area. The most notable of these is the Audit Logging plugin,[1] which exposes additional event hooks and provides automatic full-record logging functionality. There is also the Hibernate Events plugin,[2] which provides `afterInsert`, `afterUpdate`, `afterDelete`, `beforeLoad`, `afterLoad`, `beforeSave`, and `afterSave`.

Adding Functionality to Multiple Domain Classes

Although most work in GORM is done by adding functionality to individual domain classes, it is also easy to add functionality to many classes in a single declaration.

---

[1]   http://www.grails.org/Grails+Audit+Logging+Plugin

[2]   http://www.grails.org/Hibernate+Events+Plugin

Base Class Approach (Inheritance Tree)

The simplest way to add functionality to multiple domain classes is by providing a base class those classes can inherit from. Some care has to be taken in this approach, because inheriting from another domain class sets up a data inheritance structure (see "Creating and Defining Inheritance Trees" earlier in this chapter). This can be sidestepped by making the parent class abstract, although it's notable that the abstract parent's properties will be the child's table unless they are explicitly marked transient. In most cases, simply defining the transient properties on the abstract parent will do fine. If, however, there are also transient properties on the child, the child transient definition will override the abstract parent transient definition, which means the abstract parent properties will be visible again. Code Listing 1-25 demonstrates how a child class can have its own transient properties and "inherit" the parent transient properties.

Code Listing 1-25. Overriding Transient Properties While Still Including Superclass Values

```
// In ./grails-app/domain/Base.groovy
abstract class Base {
  static transients = ['base','doubleBase']
  int base
 // Any 'get' method creates artificial property
 int getDoubleBase() { 2 * base }
}


// In ./grails-app/domain/Foo.groovy
class Foo extends Base {
  static transients = Base.transients + ['workVar']

  int bar
  int workVar
}
```

Code Listing 1-26. Demonstrating Superclass Transients

```
// In ./test/integration/FooTests.groovy
  void testFooImplementsBase() {
    def foo = new Foo()
    assertTrue foo instanceof Base
    foo.base = 2
    assertEquals 4, foo.doubleBase
    foo.workVar = 3
    foo.bar = 1
    assertNotNull foo.save(flush:true)
    sessionFactory.currentSession.clear()
    foo = Foo.get(foo.id)
    assertEquals 0, foo.workVar
    assertEquals 0, foo.base
  }
```

Mixin Approach (Opt-In)

Although Groovy only allows for single inheritance, a future release of Grails will include support for adding in additional methods and fields from more than one class. This pattern is called "mixins" and is one of the most exciting features in the evolution of Groovy. Until then it was easy enough to fake mixin-style functionality: simply create an interface that holds the to-be-mixed-in method names and implementations as a map, and then apply them to the domain class's metaclass in a static initializer block.

Tip   The static initializer block is extremely under-appreciated. It gives Groovy and Grails the ability to execute code at runtime in order to configure the class. When that capability is combined with metaclass access, it provides the same kind of straightforward runtime class generation and configuration capabilities that other dynamic languages enjoy.

Code Listing 1-27. Creating a Mixin Utility

```groovy
// In ./src/groovy/MixinUtils.groovy
class MixinUtils {
  static mixin(targetMetaClass, methodMap) {
    methodMap.each {
      targetMetaClass."$it.key" = it.value
    }
  }
}
```

Code Listing 1-28. Creating an Interface of Mixins

```groovy
// In ./src/groovy/Domainutils.groovy
interface DomainUtils {
  def addedMethods = [
    doAddedMethod:{->
      return "Added method to: ${delegate.class}"
    }
  ]
}
```

Code Listing 1-29. Applying the Mixin to the Foo class

```groovy
// In ./grails-app/domain/Foo.groovy
class Foo {
  static {
    MixinUtils.mixin(Foo.metaClass,

    DomainUtils.addedMethods)
  }

  int bar
}
```

Code Listing 1-30. Demonstrating the Mixin-Created Method

```
// In ./test/integration/FooTests.groovy
void testAddedMethod() {
  assertEquals("Added method to: class Foo",
    new Foo().doAddedMethod())
}
```

This approach is extremely extensible. For instance, any class that wanted the same `doAddedMethod` could use the same static initializer line as `Foo` uses, but substituting in their own class name. The mixin interface itself can contain an entire library of mappings, and the method names can be getters and setters to create artificial properties (see "Custom Methods and Artificial Properties" earlier in this chapter).

Tip   An alternative to rolling your own mixin functionality is to use the Injecto library produced by Luke Daley (`http://www.ldaley.com/injecto/`). It works a bit differently and has cleaner user-space code. You will still have to use a static initialization block, though.

Plugin Approach (Universal)

So far, our approaches to adding functionality to domain classes have required modification of the class source. To create a new method on all domain classes, even those that we do not have source access to, we can use a plugin.

The topic of plugin development is fairly broad, but this one piece of functionality is easy to implement. First, we will generate a plugin using `grails create-plugin Eg`. This generates a plugin for us, which is basically a standard Grails application with a file containing information about the plugin itself, in this case called `./Eg/EgGrailsPlugin.groovy`. We are going to edit that file, and inside the closure named `doWithDynamicMethods`, we will add our method by working with the application domain class metaclasses.

Code Listing 1-31. Adding Methods Universally

```
// In ./Eg/GrailsPlugin.groovy
  def doWithDynamicMethods = { ctx ->
    application.domainClasses.each {
      def metaClass = it.metaClass
      metaClass.'static'.universalStaticMethod = {->
        return "Universal static method."
      }
      metaClass.universalInstanceMethod = {->
        return "Universal instance method."
      }
    }
  }
```

We can now install the plugin by moving into the root of `Eg` and executing `grails package-plugin`, and then moving back into the root of our project and executing `grails install-plugin ./Eg/grails-eg-0.1.zip`.

Once the plugin is installed, all the domain classes—even domain classes created by other plugins—will have two methods attached to them: a static `universalStaticMethod()` and an instance method, `universalInstanceMethod()`. This approach is extremely powerful. In fact this approach is almost identical to the way in which Grails attaches all the built-in methods (e.g. `Foo.get(id)`) to the domain classes.

Caution   The downside of the plugin approach is that you now have two steps to building your application: if you update your plugin definition, you will need to remove the installed version of the plugin (and its zip file) from `./plugins` and then repackage and reinstall the plugin. A slightly more straightforward but certainly more dangerous maneuver is simply to edit the plugin file located underneath `./plugins`. If you decide to take that approach, be sure your change tracking works properly and be careful that you do not accidentally delete the plugin.

Plugin Approach (Selective)

One of the advantages of using the plugin approach is that you have full programmatic control over which classes get injected and how they get used. Because the injection is part of runtime code execution, anything that can be accessed by your code at runtime could be used as class configuration. This includes reading from the file system or the database, checking for marker interfaces, or simply interrogating the static state of the class.

For instance, imagine that we wanted to inject our `universalStaticMethod` and `universalInstanceMethod` only onto all three-letter domain class names or those that have the static property `likeThreeLetter` set to `true`. We could implement that requirement by extending the code used in Code Listing 1-29 by using `org.codehaus.groovy.grails.commons.GrailsClassUtils` to query for the domain property. This code is implemented in Code Listing 1-30.

Code Listing 1-32. Example of Selective Class Modification

```groovy
// In ./Eg/EgGrailsPlugin.groovy
def doWithDynamicMethods = { ctx ->
  application.domainClasses.each {
    if(it.clazz.simpleName.length() == 3 ||
      GrailsClassUtils.getStaticPropertyValue(
        it.clazz, "likeThreeLetter"
      )
    ) {
        def metaClass = it.metaClass
        metaClass.'static'.universalStaticMethod = {->
          "Universal static method."
        }
        metaClass.universalInstanceMethod = {->
          "Universal instance method."
        }
      }
    }
  }
```

Category Approach (Lexical)

An alternative to the plugin approach is using Groovy's categories to extend domain classes. Categories offer a way to temporarily inject some useful methods into a particular segment of code. They are created by defining a library of static methods and then using a `use` block to apply the category into some space. Inside the `use` block, Groovy will not only look for methods directly on the classes, but also for a static method on the category where the first argument is the target object and the arguments are appended from there. Although this approach may seem odd to Java developers, those used to more directly C-derived object orientation will find the mapping familiar.

The major advantage to categories is that they can be defined to apply as broadly or as specifically as you would like, and categories can neatly organize related logic that applies to disparate types in a single place. The major disadvantage is that the category is lexically scoped; that is, the category has to be open directly around the code being executed—when the close bracket is hit the category is removed. Although recursing into methods works, this behavior can cause issues with closures.

Code Listing 1-33. Example of a Category Definition

```
// In ./src/groovy/SampleCategory.groovy
import org.apache.log4j.Logger

class SampleCategory {
  static void logDump(obj) {
    Logger.getLogger(obj.class).debug(
      "${obj} Dump:\n${obj.dump()}"
    )
  }
  static void logDump(Foo foo) {
    foo.log.debug(
    "Specialized Foo Dump:\n${foo.dump()}"
    )
  }
}
```

Code Listing 1-34. Demonstrating Category Definitions

```groovy
// In ./test/integration/FooTests.groovy
void logDumpViaMethod(obj) {
  obj.logDump()
}
void testDemonstrateLexicalCategoryScoping() {
  def closure
  use(SampleCategory) {
    1.logDump()
    def foo = new Foo()
    foo.logDump()
    logDumpViaMethod(foo)
    closure = { foo.logDump() }
  }
  shouldFail(MissingMethodException) {
    closure()
  }
}
```

As a general statement, the category approach should be reserved for when an entire library of functionality is used to solve isolated problems. When considering general utility methods this approach is very verbose and somewhat awkward compared to the others.

Creating Domain Classes Within Packages

Grails defaults to putting all domain classes into the root package. While most applications continue with this default, there are often reasons why you do not want to pollute the root package. One of the best reasons is because you are writing a plugin and you do not want your plugin to accidentally conflict with a name the user may already have.

Thankfully, Grails supports packaging domain classes. To generate a packaged domain class, simply qualify the name of the domain class when you execute the `grails create-domain-class foo.bar.Baz` command. This generates the domain class and integration test in the appropriate folder structure and prepends the `package` statement into the generated Groovy class.

Defining Relationships Between Classes

Building independent domain classes is a very powerful way to model the domain. However, the domain model classes will have relationships to one another, and modeling those relationships has traditionally been one of the most awkward and tricky parts of ORM solutions. Where there are some nuances in their use (see "Demystifying Association Cascades"), the basic means of constructing database relationships are fairly simple.

Has-One Relationships Using Join

The simplest kind of relationship two classes can have is for one domain class to have a reference to another domain class. This is accomplished simply enough: define a property whose type is another domain class.

Code Listing 1-35. Defining a Has-One Relationship

```
// In ./grails-app/domain/Bar.groovy
class Bar {
  int value
}


// In ./grails-app/domain/Foo.groovy
class Foo {
  Bar bar
}
```

For the most part this property is used identically to primitive properties on domain objects. The one trick is that when it comes time to save a `Foo` instance, the associated `Bar` instance needs to already been saved. The `Bar` instance need not have been flushed to the database, but it needs to be saved so that the underlying Hibernate session is aware of it. Objects that Hibernate is not aware of are called "transient", and if you see an error complaining about a transient instance, it means that you forgot to save the instance you tried to store.

Code Listing 1-36. Demonstrating Saving Dependent Records

```
// In ./test/integration/FooTest.groovy
  void testFooCanSaveWithSavedBar() {
    def foo = new Foo()
    def bar = new Bar()
    bar.value = 1
    assertNotNull bar.save()
    foo.bar = bar
    assertNotNull foo.save()
  }

  void testFooCannotSaveWithTransientBar() {
    def foo = new Foo()
    foo.bar = new Bar()
    foo.bar.value = 1
    // Note: No foo.bar.save()
    // Exception package: org.springframework.dao
    shouldFail(DataIntegrityViolationException) {
      foo.save()
    }
  }
```

Although the test in Code Listing 1-36 implies that the transient instance will get caught on save, that is not necessarily the case. It is possible that the transient instance may not be caught until the flush occurs.

Code Listing 1-37. Demonstrating Delayed Transient Detection

```
void testSaveBarAndThenSaveTransientBar() {
  def foo = new Foo()
  def bar = new Bar()
  bar.value = 1
  assertNotNull bar.save()
  foo.bar = bar
  assertNotNull foo.save()
  foo.bar = new Bar()
  bar.value = 1
  assertNotNull foo.save() // Apparently OK
  shouldFail(TransientObjectException)  {
    sessionFactory.currentSession.flush()
  }
}
```

Due to this awkwardness, if you are saving a new and potentially transient instance onto an object, you should make sure to do a flush as soon as possible. If you do not flush aggressively here, the transient object exception may occur in an apparently unrelated piece of code and it can be somewhat difficult to hunt down.

Has-One Relationships Using Composition

One of the less appreciated capabilities of GORM is the ability to hold references to nondomain Java beans. In this way you can group pieces of information that do not need their own table or GORM behaviors, but still benefit from enhanced grouping, encapsulation, and logic. This approach also saves a join on the database queries, which generally saves significant work on the side of the database.

Fields defined through composition are called "embedded", and are listed in the `embedded` static property.

Code Listing 1-38. Defining Embedded Classes

```groovy
// In ./src/groovy/Name.groovy
class Name {
  String first
  String last
  String toString() { return "$first $last" }
}
// In ./grails-app/domain/Foo.groovy
class Foo {
  static embedded = ['bar']
  Name bar
}
```

Once the embedded field is defined, it is treated in roughly the same way as a has-one field, except that you do not call `save` on the embedded instance: the embedded field is stored directly on the parent's table, so there is no distinct communication with the database or instance management.

Code Listing 1-39. Demonstrating Embedded Field Usage

```groovy
// In ./test/integration/FooTests.groovy
void testBarName() {
  def foo = new Foo()
  foo.bar = new Name()
  foo.bar.first = "Robert"
  foo.bar.last = "Fischer"
  assertEquals "Robert Fischer", foo.bar.toString()
  foo.save(flush:true)
```

```
    sessionFactory.currentSession.clear()
    foo = Foo.get(foo.id)
    assertEquals "Robert", foo.bar.first
    assertEquals "Fischer", foo.bar.last
    assertEquals "Robert Fischer", foo.bar.toString()
}
```

Bidirectional One-to-One Relationships

While you can simply treat a one-to-one relationship as two has-one relationships, that is usually not the best route to go since managing objects is more difficult when both sides of the relationship know about the other. In this case, instead of simply being able to work with one class talking to another, we need to manage a bidirectional relationship. As just one example of the problems this creates, consider the previous "Has-One Relationships Using Join" section. In that section we saw that it caused an exception to save an instance referring to a transitive instance. Both sides know about another in a bidirectional relationship, so given two transitive instances that each refers to the other, which side do you save first?

GORM handles most of this awkwardness for the user, but in order to do so the user must define one part of the relationship as the "owner" or "parent". In a one-to-one relationship, parents specify their children as properties just like in a standard has-one relationship. Children specify their owner by setting a value in the static `belongsTo` map instead of the standard has-one property.

Code Listing 1-40. Defining a One-to-One Relationship

```
// In ./grails-app/domain/Foo.groovy
class Foo {
  Bar bar
}
// In ./grails-app/domain/Bar.groovy
class Bar {
  static belongsTo = [parent:Foo]
}
```

In the previous code listing, the `Foo` class is the parent of the `Bar` class, hence, `Bar belongsTo Foo`. Once these classes are defined, the child class (`Bar`) can be treated basically as though it were embedded; the parent class (`Foo`) will manage saving the child class. Notably, the reverse is not true—saving the child class will not save the parent class.

Code Listing 1-41. Demonstrating a One-to-One Relationship

```
// In ./test/integration/FooTests.groovy
void testFooOwningBarCanSave() {
  def foo = new Foo()
  foo.bar = new Bar()
  assertNotNull foo.save(flush:true)
  assertNotNull foo.bar.id
  assertNull foo.bar.parent
  def fooId = foo.id
  def barId = foo.bar.id
  foo = null
  sessionFactory.currentSession.clear()
  foo = Foo.get(fooId)
  assertEquals foo.bar.id, barId
  assertNull foo.bar.parent
```

Grails Persistence with GORM and GSQL

```
  }

  void testBarCannotSaveFoo() {
    def bar = new Bar()
    bar.parent = new Foo()
    shouldFail(InvalidDataAccessApiUsageException) {
      bar.save(flush:true)
    }
  }

  void testSettingParentOnBarDoesNotSetFoo() {
    def bar = new Bar()
    bar.parent = new Foo()
    assertNull bar.parent.bar
  }
```

In the previous code listing, we see that although we set the child property on our parent class, the parent property on the child class is not set. This is a common stumbling block for developers new to Grails, often resulting in cries of GORM's inadequacy. However, there are two good reasons for this behavior: first, it is easy to add code that automatically performs the set; second, it is possible that the appropriate property to set may not be obvious.

Code Listing 1-42. Defining and Demonstrating Automatic Assignment of Child Property's Parent Property

```
// In ./grails-app/domain/Foo.groovy
class Foo {
  Bar bar
  void setBar(newBar) {
    bar = newBar
    bar.parent = this
```

```
    }
}


// In ./test/integration/FooTests.groovy
void testFooOwningBarCanSave() {
    def foo = new Foo()
    foo.bar = new Bar()
    assertNotNull foo.save(flush:true)
    assertNotNull foo.bar.id
    assertNotNull foo.bar.parent
    def fooId = foo.id
    def barId = foo.bar.id
    foo = null
    sessionFactory.currentSession.clear()
    foo = Foo.get(fooId)
    assertEquals foo.bar.id, barId
    assertNotNull foo.bar.parent
}
```

Code Listing 1-43. Demonstrating Problem with Auto-Assignment

```
// If two properties of the same type are
// specified, which should be set?


// In ./grails-app/domain/Foo.groovy
class Foo {
  Bar bar
}
// In ./grails-app/domain/Bar.groovy
class Bar {
   static belongsTo = [parent1:Foo, parent2:Foo]
}
```

One-to-Many Relationships

Defining a one-to-many relationship in GORM is only a single step beyond the one-to-one relationship. The parent class, instead of having a simple property that links to the child, has a static `hasMany` property. That property is a map of the collection name onto the type of the child objects. The parent is still responsible for managing the relationship, and so saving the parent will save the child, but not vice versa.

Code Listing 1-44. Defining a One-to-Many Relationship

```
// In ./grails-app/domain/Foo.groovy
class Foo {
  static hasMany = [bars:Bar]
}
// In ./grails-app/domain/Bar.groovy
class Bar {
  static belongsTo = [parent:Foo]
}
```

Code Listing 1-45. Demonstrating a One-to-Many Relationship

```
// In ./test/integration/FooTests.groovy
  void testFooSavingManyBars() {
    def foo = new Foo()
    assertNull foo.bars
    foo.save()
    foo.bars = []
    foo.bars << new Bar()
    foo.bars << new Bar()
    foo.bars << new Bar()
    foo.bars.each { it.parent = foo }
    assertNotNull foo.save(flush:true)
    assertEquals 3, foo.bars.size()
  }
```

The `hasMany` declaration implicitly creates a `Collection` property with the association's name (`bars` in this case) that elements can be added to and removed from. That collection is saved when the parent object itself is saved.

The default behavior of that property is to be a `Set`, and therefore to not have any guarantied ordering from the elements. If you want to be somewhat more explicit about the order of the elements, you can create the field with an explicit kind of collection. Most popular for fixing the order of the elements in the collection are `List` and `SortedSet`.

Code Listing 1-46. Defining `List` and `SortedSet` Relationships

```
// In ./grails-app/domain/Bar.groovy
class Bar {
  static belongsTo = [parent:Foo]
}
// In ./grails-app/domain/Baz.groovy
class Baz implements Comparable {
  static belongsTo = [parent: Foo]
  int value
  int compareTo(Object them) {
    return this.value <=> them.value
  }
}
// In ./grails-app/domain/Foo.groovy
class Foo {
  static hasMany = [bars:Bar, bazzes:Baz]
  List bars
  SortedSet bazzes
}
```

In the sorted set relationship (the `bazzes` relationship) the child domain class needs to implement `Comparable`. Implementing that interface provides a natural ordering to the class, which is used to determine the sorting of the elements. At this point there is no support for using external or custom comparators on domain classes in GORM.

Code Listing 1-47. Demonstrating `List` and `SortedSet` Relationships

```
// In ./test/integration/FooTests.groovy
void testFooSavingBarList() {
  def foo = new Foo()
  assertNull foo.bars
  foo.save()
  foo.bars = []
  foo.bars << new Bar()
  foo.bars << new Bar()
  foo.bars << new Bar()
  foo.bars.each { it.parent = foo }
  assertNotNull foo.save(flush:true)
  def barIds = foo.bars*.id
  sessionFactory.currentSession.clear()
  foo = Foo.get(foo.id)
  assertEquals 3, foo.bars.size()
  assertTrue foo.bars instanceof List
  barIds.eachWithIndex { it, idx ->
    assertEquals it, foo.bars[idx].id
  }
}

  void testFooSavingBazzesSortedSet() {
    def foo = new Foo()
```

```
assertNull foo.bazzes
foo.save()
foo.bazzes = [] as SortedSet
(1..3).each {
  def baz = new Baz()
  baz.value = -1 * it
  foo.bazzes << baz
}
foo.bazzes.each {
  assertNull it.parent
  it.parent = foo
}
assertNotNull foo.save(flush:true)
def bazIds = foo.bazzes*.id
sessionFactory.currentSession.clear()
foo = Foo.get(foo.id)
assertEquals 3, foo.bazzes.size()
assertTrue foo.bazzes instanceof SortedSet
def bazList = foo.bazzes as List
bazIds.eachWithIndex { it, idx ->
  assertEquals it, bazList[idx].id
}
}
```

Many-to-Many Relationships

The way GORM handles many-to-many relationships is basically a natural progression of the one-to-many relationship. This means that although there may not be a semantic parent/child relationship, one side of the relationship needs to accept the role of child, and the parent is the one that manages the relationship.

To implement a many-to-many relationship, simply add a `hasMany` declaration to the child. The `belongsTo` declaration on the child still sticks around. GORM manages all the back-end database bookkeeping involved in the many-to-many relationship, including creating and managing the association table.

Code Listing 1-48. Defining a Many-to-Many Relationship

```
// In ./grails-app/domain/Foo.groovy
class Foo {
  static hasMany = [bars:Bar, bazzes:Baz ]
  SortedSet bazzes
}
// In ./grails-app/domain/Bar.groovy
class Bar {
  static belongsTo = Foo
  static hasMany = [parents:Foo]
}
// In ./grails-app/domain/Baz.groovy
class Baz implements Comparable {
  static belongsTo = Foo
  static hasMany = [parents:Foo]
  int value
  int compareTo(Object them) {
    return this.value <=> them.value
  }
}
```

Code Listing 1-49. Demonstrating a Many-to-Many Relationship

```groovy
// In ./test/integration/FooTests.groovy
  void testManyToManyBarsAndBazzes() {
      def foo = new Foo()
      foo.bars = []
      (1..4).each { foo.addToBars(new Bar()) }
      foo.bazzes = [] as SortedSet
      (1..3).each {
        def baz = new Baz()
        baz.value = it
        foo.addToBazzes(baz)
      }
      assertEquals 4, foo.bars.size()
      assertEquals 3, foo.bazzes.size()
      assertNotNull foo.save(flush:true)
      sessionFactory.currentSession.clear()
      foo = Foo.get(foo.id)
      assertEquals 4, foo.bars.size()
      assertEquals 3, foo.bazzes.size()
  }
```

Unlike a one-to-many relationship, the many-to-many relationship does not support the List collection type. There is no particularly good reason that List is not supported, and there is an outstanding request to extend GORM to support List collections. In the mean time, the same functionality can be kludged in by specifying a SortedSet and managing your own indexes.

Code Listing 1-50. Simulating a List on Many-to-Many Relationships

```groovy
// In ./grails-app/domain/Foo.groovy
class Foo {
  static hasMany = [bars:Bar, bazzes:Baz ]
  SortedSet bars,bazzes
  void addToBars(bar) {
    bar.fooIdx = bars.fold(0) { memo,nextBar ->
      Math.max(memo, nextBar.fooIdx)
    }
    bars << bar
  }
}
// In ./grails-app/domain/Bar.groovy
class Bar implements Comparable {
  static belongsTo = Foo
  static hasMany = [parents:Foo]
  int fooIdx
  int compareTo(them) {
    this.fooIdx <=> them.fooIdx ?:
    this.id <=> them.id        ?:
    this.hashCode() <=> them.hashCode()
  }
}
```

Code Listing 1-51. Demonstrating Many-to-Many Simulated List Behavior

```groovy
// In ./test/integration/FooTests.groovy
  void testManyToManyBarsAsList() {
      def foo = new Foo()
      foo.bars = [] as SortedSet
      (1..4).each { foo.addToBars(new Bar()) }
      assertEquals 4, foo.bars.size()
      assertNotNull foo.save(flush:true)
      def ids = foo.bars*.id
      sessionFactory.currentSession.clear()
      foo = Foo.get(foo.id)
      assertEquals 4, foo.bars.size()
      def bars = foo.bars as List
      ids.eachWithIndex { id, idx ->
        assertEquals id, bars[idx].id
      }
  }
```

Defining Tree Relationships

A tree structure is a very common but often-neglected relationship. A model with a tree structure is one that holds references to other objects of the same type. Tree structures appear frequently in social media sites, such as message board posts with responses, users that have "friends," or web sites that reference others.

The simplest way to represent a tree structure in GORM is as a many-to-many relationship where both sides of the many-to-many are the same type. In short this means that you use the hasMany property but point to your own type. The functionality provided by the belongsTo property is provided for free.

Code Listing 1-52. Defining a Has-Many Tree Relationship

```
// In ./grails-app/domain/Foo.groovy
class Foo {
    static hasMany = [children:Foo]
}
```

Code Listing 1-53. Demonstrating a Has-Many Tree Relationship

```
// In ./test/integration/FooTests.groovy
void testFooHasChildren() {
    def foo1 = new Foo()
    def foo2 = new Foo()
    assertNull foo1.children
    foo1.children = [foo2]
    assertNotNull foo1.save(flush:true)
    sessionFactory.currentSession.clear()
    foo1 = Foo.get(foo1.id)
    assertEquals 1, foo1.children.size()
    assertTrue foo1.children*.id.contains(foo2.id)
}
```

Intermediaries and Has-Many-Through Relationships

Although a many-to-many relationship is a convenient shorthand, often the many-to-many relationship itself becomes a part of the domain. For instance, consider the case of a web site where users can mark a piece of content as "liked." A user can like many pieces of content, and a piece of content can be liked by many users, so this is a many-to-many relationship. However, it would not be surprising if the relationship itself begins to collect data such as when it was created or some categorization by the user. In this case, the many-to-many relationship is broken into two many-to-one relationships over a linking object: a content and a user each have many links, and a link has one content and one user. This relationship pattern has come to be called a "has-many-through" relationship.

There is no innate support for has-many-through relationships in GORM. However, the pattern for supporting has-many-through is straightforward: simply follow the pattern of the has-one relationships and add a few helper methods.

Code Listing 1-54. Defining a Has-Many-Through Relationship

```
// In ./grails-app/domain/Link.groovy
class Link {
  static belongsTo = [foo:Foo, bar:Bar]
}
// In ./grails-app/domain/Foo.groovy
class Foo {
  static hasMany = [links:Link]
  def getBars() { links*.bar }
  def addToBars(bar) {
    bar.save() // Prevents transient instance issue
    def link = new Link()
    link.bar = bar
    bar.addToLinks(link)
    this.addToLinks(link)
  }
}
// In ./grails-app/domain/Bar.groovy
class Bar {
  static hasMany = [links:Link]
  def getFoos() { links*.foo }
  def addToFoos(foo) {
```

```
    foo.save()   // Prevents transient instance isssue
    foo.addToBars(this)
  }
}
```

Code Listing 1-55. Demonstrating a Has-Many-Through Relationship

```
// In ./test/integration/FooTests.groovy
void testFooLinkBar() {
  def foo = new Foo()
  foo.save()
  def bar = new Bar()
  bar.save()
  def link = new Link()
  foo.addToLinks(link)
  bar.addToLinks(link)
  link.save()
  sessionFactory.currentSession.flush()
  sessionFactory.currentSession.clear()
  foo = Foo.get(foo.id)
  assertEquals 1, foo.links.size()
  def newLink = (foo.links as List)[0]
  assertEquals link.id, newLink.id
  assertEquals bar.id, newLink.bar.id
  assertEquals 1, newLink.bar.links.size()
  newLink = (newLink.bar.links as List)[0]
  assertEquals foo.id, newLink.foo.id
}

void testFooBar() {
  def foo = new Foo()
  foo.addToBars(new Bar())
```

```
    assertNotNull foo.save(flush:true)
    def barId = (foo.bars as List)[0].id
    assertFalse 0 == barId
    assertNotNull barId
    sessionFactory.currentSession.clear()
    foo = Foo.get(foo.id)
    assertEquals 1, foo.bars.size()
    def bar = (foo.bars as List)[0]
    assertEquals bar.id, bar.id
    assertEquals 1, bar.foos.size()
    assertEquals foo.id, (bar.foos as List)[0].id
}
```

Constructing New Instances

The constructor is the key method in Java and it gets a lot of play in
GORM. Through the GORM constructor, domain objects are automatically
provided with a set of dynamic properties and methods and hooks into the
underlying Hibernate structures. In addition to the default, no-argument
constructor, GORM overloads the constructor with a map-based
implementation. The constructor that takes a map can be used to define
properties of the GORM during construction. Keys in the map correspond
to property names, and values in the map correspond to property values
(more details are provided in the topics that follow). Thanks to the magic of
Groovy, you can even write the map without the surrounding square
brackets, reminiscent of named arguments.

This magic comes at a price. Because of the amount of magic that Groovy
and GORM put into the constructor, the GORM user should only be using
the constructor and not trying to redefine it. Although there is a well-
intentioned temptation to put initialization logic into the constructor, that is
almost certainly the wrong answer in GORM: property defaults should be
defined inline (see the previous "Default Property Values" section) and

complex initialization logic should go into the `onLoad` handler (see the "Events" section earlier in this chapter).

Setting Basic Properties via Map Constructor

Basic properties are set on GORM via the same map constructor structure that is available to any Groovy bean. Arguments can be passed as an implicit map or by passing an explicit map to the constructor. This constructor will assign properties to the values in the map, including artificial properties and properties with overridden setters.

Code Listing 1-56. Demonstrating Setting Properties via the Map Constructor

```
// In ./grails-app/domain/Foo.groovy
class Foo {
  int integer
  String string
  double otherValue
  def setOtherValue(val) {
    this.@otherValue =
Double.parseDouble(val.toString())
  }
}
// In ./test/integration/FooTests.groovy
void testAssignSimplePropertiesImplicitMap() {
    def foo = new Foo(
                    string:'grok',
                    integer:42,
                    otherValue:'3.14'
                    )
    assertEquals 'grok', foo.string
    assertEquals 42, foo.integer
```

```
        assertEquals 3.14, foo.otherValue
    }
    void testAssignSimplePropertiesExplicitMap() {
        def map = [
                    string:'grok',
                    integer:42,
                    otherValue:'3.14'
                    ]
        def foo = new Foo(map)
        assertEquals 'grok', foo.string
        assertEquals 42, foo.integer
        assertEquals 3.14, foo.otherValue
    }
    void testSimplePropertiesPropertiesClone() {
        def source = new Foo(
                        string:'grok',
                        integer:42,
                        otherValue:3.14
                        )
        def target = new Foo(source.properties)
        assertEquals 'grok', target.string
        assertEquals 42, target.integer
        assertEquals 3.14, target.otherValue
    }
```

Setting Relationship Properties via Map Constructor

The map constructor, however, is not limited to setting simple properties.
Relationship values can also be set via the map constructor by passing in a
GPath expression as the map key. In order for this to work, the properties
have to be initialized to non-null default values.

Code Listing 1-57. Demonstrating Setting Relationship Properties

```groovy
// In ./grails-app/domain/Foo.groovy
class Foo {
  static embedded = ['name']
  static hasMany = [bazzes:Baz]
  Name name = new Name()
  Bar bar = new Bar()
}
// In ./grails-app/domain/Bar.groovy
class Bar {
  int value
}
// In ./grails-app/domain/Baz.groovy
class Baz { }
// In ./src/groovy/Name.groovy
class Name {
  String first, last
}
// In ./test/integration/FooTests.groovy
  void testSetEmbeddedProperty() {
    def name = new Name(first:'First',last:'Last')
    def foo = new Foo(name:name)
    assertEquals name.first, foo.name.first
    assertEquals name.last, foo.name.last
  }

  void testSetEmbeddedPropertyValues() {
    def foo = new Foo(
      'name.first':'First',
      'name.last':'Last'
```

```
    )
    assertTrue foo.name instanceof Name
    assertEquals 'First', foo.name.first
    assertEquals 'Last', foo.name.last
}

void testSetOneToOnePropertyValues() {
    def foo = new Foo('bar.value':1)
    assertTrue foo.bar instanceof Bar
    assertEquals 1, foo.bar.value
}

void testSetManyPropertyCollection() {
    def bazzes = [new Baz(), new Baz(), new Baz()]
    def foo = new Foo(bazzes:bazzes)
    assertEquals 3, foo.bazzes.size()
}
```

Chapter 2: Customizing GORM Mapping and Enforcing Data Integrity

Data Integrity Through Constraints

While the structure of the domain class is important, it is only part of the story in domain modeling. Equally as critical to the domain model is data integrity—without ensuring data integrity the domain model will quickly degrade into nonsense. When the model degrades in this way the application as a whole degrades as well. The invariants the application is built on break down and surprising exceptions pop up, resulting in application failures.

To prevent this breakdown, GORM provides validation via constraints. These constraints limit the acceptable value of a property and provide the basic away to enforce data integrity in the model. In addition, GORM will leverage these constraints to guide the creation of the automatically generated DDL.

Specifying Constraints

In GORM, constraints are specified through the `constraints` static property. That property is assigned a closure that is then executed as a DSL. The domain class properties become method names and the arguments are the constraints to apply to the properties.

The constraints report their error messages through an internationalization support structure (i18n). This may seem like unnecessary and surprising overhead to a web development newcomer, but there is significant wisdom behind that approach.

In addition to the obvious advantage of being able to deliver localized error messages, the internationalization layer also provides a clean break between the presentation of the error message and the error message itself, akin to the clean break between controllers and views: the constraint can worry only about the logic behind the error message and leave rendering the appropriate text to the internationalization layer.

Built-In Data Constraints

Grails provides a long list of simple constraints that can be applied to simple data properties. These properties act in fairly self-descriptive ways to limit properties.

Code Listing 2-1. Demonstrating Some Simple Data Constraints

```
// In ./grails-app/domain/Foo.groovy
class Foo {
  String userName
  String email
  String homePage
  String userType
  int loginCount
  static constraints = {
    userName(unique:true, matches:/\w+/)
    email(email:true)
    homePage(url:true)
    userType(inList:['USER','ADMIN'])
    loginCount(min:0)
  }
}
  // In ./test/integration/FooTests.groovy
  Foo generateFoo() {
    return new Foo(
      userName:'Robert', email:'robert@email.com',
      homePage:'http://smokejumperit.com',
```

```
      userType:'ADMIN', loginCount:1
  )
}
void testRawGeneratedFooWorks() {
  assertNotNull generateFoo().save(flush:true)
}
void testDuplicateNameFails() {
  def foo = generateFoo()
  assertNotNull foo.save()
  foo = generateFoo()
  assertFalse foo.validate()
  def errors = foo.errors
  assertNotNull errors.getFieldError('userName')
}
void testBadNameFails() {
  def foo = generateFoo()
  foo.userName = '!@#$%^&*()'
  assertFalse foo.validate()
  def errors = foo.errors
  assertNotNull errors.getFieldError('userName')
}
void testNotEmailFails() {
  def foo = generateFoo()
  foo.email = 'not_an_email)(*&^%$%!'
  assertFalse foo.validate()
  def errors = foo.errors
  assertNotNull errors.getFieldError('email')
}
void testNotUrlFails() {
  def foo = generateFoo()
  foo.homePage = 'not_a_url)(!@%!%'
```

```
      assertFalse foo.validate()
      def errors = foo.errors
      assertNotNull errors.getFieldError('homePage')
    }
    void testNotInListUserType() {
      def foo = generateFoo()
      foo.userType = 'bad user type'
      assertFalse foo.validate()
      def errors = foo.errors
      assertNotNull errors.getFieldErrors('userType')
    }
    void testNegativeLoginCountFails() {
      def foo = generateFoo()
      foo.loginCount = -1
      assertFalse foo.validate()
      def errors = foo.errors
      assertNotNull errors.getFieldErrors('loginCount')
    }
```

The official list of validations is maintained as part of the Grails Framework Reference Documentation. Table 2-1 outlines the constraints supported by Grails as of this writing.

The `unique` property requires slightly more explanation than the table can provide. In all three forms, the property is specifying that a value must be unique—the difference is in scope.

In the Boolean form (e.g. `unique:true`) the property must be unique across all instances. In the String form (e.g. `unique: 'userType'`) the property must be unique across all instances where the value of the named property is the same as this instance's value. That is, the property must be unique within the context of another property.

In the list form (e.g. `unique:['userType', 'loginCount']`) the property must be unique across all instances where the values of all listed properties are the same as this instance's value. That is, the property must be unique within the context of a combination of other properties.

In all these cases it's possible that transactional interference can cause the uniqueness validation to succeed but the record to still fail to be committed. The issue is fundamentally one of database concurrency structures, so the only way around it is to use the debilitating non-concurrent `SERIALIZABLE` transaction isolation level. Most users find it better to simply handle the possible exception at commit time.

Table 2-1. Constraints Supported by Grails

CONSTRAINT	PROPERTY TYPE	ARGUMENT TYPE	SCHEMA	NOTES
Blank	String	Boolean	No	`false` prevents empty or whitespace only values
creditCard	String	Boolean	No	`true` validates if the value is a reasonable credit card number[3]
Email	String	Boolean	No	Use `true` for basic email structure checks
inList	Any	List	Yes	Ensures value in argument list
matches	String	regex or String	No	Entire value must match regex

---

[3] Algorithm overview is available at `http://www.merriampark.com/anatomycc.htm` (not modifiable via a plugin although similar checks can be done through the validator constraint).

Table 2-1. Constraints Supported by Grails (continued)

Constraint	Property Type	Argument Type	Schema	Notes
max	Comparable	Same	Yes	Ensures that value <= argument
maxSize	String or Collection	Integer	Yes	For String, limits length; for Collection, limits element count
Min	Comparable	Same	Yes	Ensures that value >= argument
minSize	String or Collection	Integer	Yes	For String, limits length; for Collection, limits element count
notEqual	Any	Same	No	Ensures value != argument
nullable	Any	Boolean	Yes	`true` allows `null` values
range	Comparable	Range	Yes	Convenience for min/max
scale	float, double, or BigDecimal	Integer	Yes	Number of digits to the right of the decimal point
size	String or Collection	Range	Yes	Convenience for minSize and maxSize; cannot use with blank or nullable
unique (Boolean)	Any	Boolean	Yes	Use `true` to require a unique value

Table 2-1. Constraints Supported by Grails (continued)

CONSTRAINT	PROPERTY TYPE	ARGUMENT TYPE	SCHEMA	NOTES
unique (String)	Any	String (property name)	Yes	Value must be unique within argument property
unique (List)	Any	List of Strings	Yes	Must be unique within property combination
url	String	Boolean	No	Use `true` to perform basic URL checks

Note   The Schema column in this table denotes whether or not the row's constraint affects the schema generated by GORM's `hbm2ddl`—that is, whether or not the constraint is reflected in the database in some way.

Custom Constraints

Sooner or later an application model will become advanced enough where simple constraints fail to capture some nuance of the data. Given the apparent inevitability of this complexity, it is surprising to see that many previous ORMs required an extensive amount of coding and configuration in order to implement new constraints and make them.

In GORM, a custom constraint is implemented by using the `validator` key on the argument map. That key takes a closure as a value, and the closure executes the evaluation. Details of the closure's behavior are extremely variable but fall into basically two camps: the three argument form and the zero, one, and two argument form.

The zero, one, and two argument form takes up to two optional arguments. The first argument is the value of the property. If the closure is looking for a second argument, the second argument is the object holding that property. In addition, the name of the property being validated is provided via the `propertyName` variable.

For return values the closure can return either `true` or `null` to indicate a valid value, or it can return `false` to indicate a generic invalid value. Alternatively, the validator can leverage the internationalization structure (`i18n`) and return a String. That String is appended to `classname.propertyname.` to form the message key.

If additional information is needed for the internationalization message, the validator can go even further and return a List. The List should consist of a String, which is appended to `classname.propertyname.` to form the message key as before, and can follow with as many additional parameters to the message as the user would like. For examples of how these messages look and how to define them, see the file located at `./grails-app/i18n/messages.properties` and the associated language files in that folder.

Code Listing 2-2. Demonstrating Basic Validators

```
// In ./grails-app/domain/Foo.groovy
class Foo {
  String oneArgValue = "One", twoArgValue = "Two"
  boolean skipTwoArgCheck = true,
          msgValue = true,
          listValue = true
  static constraints = {
    oneArgValue(validator:{ return it == "One" })
    twoArgValue(validator:{ val, obj ->
      return obj.skipTwoArgCheck ||
             val == "Two"
  })
    msgValue(validator:{
      if(!it) { return "my.msg.key" }
```

```
    })
    listValue(validator:{
      if(!it) {
        return ["my.other.msg.key","blue",42]
      }
    })
  }
}
# From ./grails-app/i18n/messages.properties
foo.msgValue.my.msg.key=From messages.properties
foo.listValue.my.other.msg.key=[{0}][{1}][{2}][{3}][{4}]
// From ./test/integration/FooTests.groovy
  void testSuccessfulSave() {
    assertNotNull new Foo().save(flush:true)
  }
  void testOneArgFailure() {
    def foo = new Foo()
    foo.oneArgValue = "Not One"
    assertFalse foo.validate()
    def errs = foo.errors
    def error = errs.getFieldError("oneArgValue")
    assertNotNull error
  }
  void testTwoArgFailure() {
    def foo = new Foo(
                skipTwoArgCheck:false,
                twoArgValue:'Not Two'
    )
    assertFalse foo.validate()
    def errs = foo.errors
    def error = errs.getFieldError("twoArgValue")
```

```
        assertNotNull error
        assertNull errs.getFieldError("skipTwoArgCheck")
    }
    String messageForError(error) {
        messageSource.getMessage(error, Locale.default)
    }
    void testMsgValueMessage() {
        def foo = new Foo(msgValue:false)
        assertFalse foo.validate()
        def error = foo.errors.getFieldError("msgValue")
        assertEquals "From messages.properties",
                     messageForError(error)
    }
    void testListValueMessage() {
        def foo = new Foo(listValue:false)
        assertFalse foo.validate()
        def errs = foo.errors
        def error = errs.getFieldError("listValue")
        assertEquals(
          "[listValue][class Foo][false][blue][42]",
          messageForError(error)
        )
    }
```

The three argument form is for serious GORM power users. As in the zero,
one, and two argument forms, the first two arguments are the value and the
object being validated. The third argument is the object's `errors` object
itself. Instead of checking for a return value, the closure is expected to
modify the `errors` object directly to reflect the state of any errors. This
errors object is an instance of `org.springframework.validation.`
`Errors`, and the user can leverage that full API to specify all kinds of

special or complex error logic, including the ability to create global errors as opposed to field errors.

Code Listing 2-3. Demonstrating Global Errors via Validator

```
// In ./grails-app/domain/Foo.groovy
class Foo {
  boolean failMe = false
  static constraints = {
    failMe(validator:{ val,obj,err ->
      if(val) { err.reject("failed") }
    })
  }
}
# From ./grails-app/i18n/messages.properties
failed=Globally failed!


// In ./test/integration/FooTests.groovy
  String messageForError(error) {
    messageSource.getMessage(error, Locale.default)
  }
  void testFailMeTrueIsGlobalError() {
    def foo = new Foo(failMe:true)
    assertFalse foo.validate()
    def error = foo.errors.globalError
    assertNotNull error
    assertEquals "Globally failed!",
                 messageForError(error)
  }
```

Customizing the Object/Relational Mapping

GORM provides extensive functionality to customize the mapping, including structural customizations to map GORM objects onto legacy tables or to nudge GORM into conformance with corporate standards or personal sensibilities. These customizations also include functional changes that tweak GORM's default behavior to improve performance in each particular case. All of this customization is done by assigning a closure to the `mapping` static property and setting values within the inline DSL it provides.

Custom and Escaped Table Names

The table name used for a domain object can be specified by calling the `table` method provided by the mapping DSL. The value is used directly as the table name in the underlying SQL. In this way, chatty table name requirements can be mapped into succinct domain object names.

Code Listing 2-4. Customizing a Table Name

```
// In ./grails-app/domain/Foo.groovy
class Foo {
  static mapping = {
    table 't_gorm_book_foo'
  }
}
```

Escaping the table name is a special case of table name mapping. One of the most common problems reported back to Grails is that after creating a domain class with a name such as `Call` or `Group`, Hibernate will fail to create the table or will error out on efforts to insert or query onto it. The result may be an error on start-up complaining about unexpected tokens, or an `InvalidDataAccessResourceUsageException` or `SQLGrammarException`. This behavior variance originates from how permissive different databases are; even within the same database, using keywords can change wildly even from keyword to keyword.

This wide range of behaviors makes identifying this issue somewhat tricky, but once it has been identified, fixing it is simple: just add backticks to your table name. Hibernate will translate the backticks into the appropriate escaping for your database.

Code Listing 2-5. Escaping a Table Name

```
// In ./grails-app/domain/Group.groovy
class Group {
  static mapping = {
    table "`group`"
  }
}
```

Customizing Properties

The DSL parts for property customization strongly resemble the DSL for constraints. Inside the `mapping` closure, you customize a property's mapping behavior by calling a method with the property name and passing named arguments.

Customizing the Underlying Column Name

The name of the column underlying the property type can be set with the `column` key. As with table names (see the previous topic), you can use backticks to escape the SQL reserved words surrounding the column name.

Code Listing 2-6. Customizing Column Names

```
// In ./grails-app/domain/Foo.groovy
class Foo {
  String value
  int order
  static mapping = {
    value column:'s_value'
    order column:'`order`'
  }
}
```

Customizing Type: Basic Hibernate Types

While the default types specified by GORM are often sufficient for most applications undergoing development, it is not uncommon for the user to need to change the default types. In particular, in any case where an entire text document is being stored (e.g. wiki pages), the Hibernate `text` type is probably preferable over the `varchar` type. Date properties are also strong candidates for adjustment.

To adjust the type, use the unsurprisingly named `type` key with a string value that is the name of the Hibernate property.

Code Listing 2-7. Specifying the Column Type of a Property

```
// In ./grails-app/domain/Foo.groovy
class Foo {
  String value = ""
  Date time = new Date()
  static mapping = {
    value type:'text'
    time type:'time'
  }
}
```

Table 2-2. Java, Hibernate, and SQL Type Cross-Reference

JAVA TYPE	HIBERNATE TYPE	SQL TYPE
int, Integer	integer	Vendor-specific numeric
long, Long	long	Vendor-specific numeric
short, Short	short	Vendor-specific numeric
float, Float	float	Vendor-specific numeric
double, Double	double	Vendor-specific numeric
char, Character	character	Vendor-specific numeric
byte, Byte	byte	Vendor-specific numeric
boolean, Boolean	yes_no, true_false	Vendor-specific Boolean
String	string	VARCHAR[4]
Date	date	DATE
Date	time	TIME
Date	timestamp	TIMESTAMP
Calendar	calendar	TIMESTAMP
Calendar	calendar_date	DATE
BigDecimal	big_decimal	Vendor-specific numeric
BigInteger	big_integer	Vendor-specific numeric

---

[4] In this table, the key VARCHAR is used to mean the VARCHAR column type on every RDBMS except Oracle. On Oracle, VARCHAR means VARCHAR2.

Table 2-2. Java, Hibernate, and SQL Type Cross-Reference (continued)

JAVA TYPE	HIBERNATE TYPE	SQL TYPE
Locale	locale	VARCHAR (ISO code)
TimeZone	timezone	VARCHAR (Java ID)
Currency	currency	VARCHAR (ISO code)
Class	class	VARCHAR (fully-qualified name)
byte[]	binary	vendor-specific binary type
String	text	TEXT/CLOB
Serializable	serializable	Vendor-specific binary type

There are a few other Hibernate types (e.g. `clob`, `blob`, `imm_binary`) but the functionality is redundant with the types listed here and their support is inconsistent. The other types should generally be avoided.

Customizing Type: User-Defined Types

If your column storage needs are more advanced than the existing Hibernate types can support, begin by considering whether your needs can be met by embedded types (see "Has-One Relationships Using Composition" in Chapter 1). If not, there is one last resort for complex type specification: Hibernate user types. A Hibernate user type provides full control over moving types to and from the database, but at the cost of much more extensive coding.

To implement a new Hibernate user type, the type must implement the interface `org.hibernate.usertype.UserType`. This consists of defining ways to translate the type to and from a `Serializable` instance; how to read, write, and update the type from the underlying JDBC structures,; and then specifying the SQL type(s) on which the new Hibernate user type is based. These requirements are well-explained in the Hibernate JavaDoc.

A Hibernate user type is specified in the same way as a base type: assign the value to the type argument of the property call in the mapping DSL. Assuming the existence of a `PostCodeType` that maps to a `String` on the Java side, it would look like the following code listing.

Code Listing 2-8. Using a Hibernate User Type for a Column

```
// In ./grails-app/domain/Foo.groovy
class Foo {
  String postCode
  static mapping = {
    postCode type:PostCodeType
  }
}
```

Customizing the Identity Column

GORM gives substantial control over the way identity is managed. The simplest and most natural control is of the identity column itself—to rename the column the `id` property is mapped to, simply specify its new name via the `column` argument like any other property.

You may also change the way that `id`s are generated by plugging in alternative Hibernate ID generators using the `generator` and `params` arguments of `id`. The default implementation is Hibernate's `native`, which uses either auto-generation or sequences depending on the predilection of the underlying database. For more information on Hibernate identity algorithms, see Table 2-3.

Code Listing 2-9. Customizing the Identity Column Name and Generation Strategy

```
// In ./grails-app/domain/Foo.groovy
class Foo {
  static mapping = {
    id column:'foo_id',
      generator:'hilo', params:[table:'keygen',
                                 column:'next',
                                 max_lo:1000]
  }
}
```

Table 2-3. Hibernate Identity Algorithms

IDENTITY ALGORITHM	DESCRIPTION
increment	Numeric ID that counts up. Not safe if more than one process is doing inserts.
identity	Use the identity column type. Not all databases have such a column type.
sequence	Use a sequence on the database. Not all databases support sequences.
hilo	Use a table in the database to generate values efficiently.
seqhilo	Use a sequence in the database to generate values efficiently.
uuid	Generated identifier of 32 hexadecimal characters that is unique within the context of a network. id is based on IP address, startup time of the JVM, system time, and a counter value.

Table 2-3. Hibernate Identity Algorithms (continued)

IDENTITY ALGORITHM	DESCRIPTION
guid	Uses the database GUID type. Not all databases have such a column type.
native	Picks one of `identity`, `sequence`, or `hilo` based on support.
assigned	Hands off responsibility for ID generation to the user.
select	Uses a select on a database trigger to produce a primary key.
Foreign	Intended for one-to-one primary key relationships, this uses the identifier of an associated object.

Using Natural Identity

Through years of collective experience, the software industry has developed a standard approach to handling databases rows: each row is identified using a column with a meaningless but guaranteed unique value, called the *artificial identifier*. This value is usually an incrementing number or some kind of generated universal ID (also known as a UUID or GUID).

The value of this approach is that it leaves the model subject to flexible changes. While a particular column or set of columns may be treated as necessarily unique today, new discoveries about the domain tomorrow may reveal that they are not actually unique.[5] If the database is structured around these newly-nonunique values, major structural changes are now required. Defaulting to artificial identifiers throughout the database is generally considered the best practice.

---

[5] The author himself has made this mistake. On a contract with a health insurance company, he once assumed that a social security number would be unique, only to discover that clients would use artificial or erroneous numbers with disturbing regularity. Lesson learned: "Business invariants always change."

Still, there is overhead to artificial identifiers, and there are times when a column really will be unique. This is often the case when some external force is defining an encoding scheme over a domain. Examples include the United States government's state abbreviations (e.g. "MN" for Minnesota) or the ISO 639 language codes (e.g. "de" for German). In these cases, using a natural identifier can result in more meaningful foreign key columns, which can save a select query if the code is the only thing desired.

Retrieving the `id` property from a lazily-initialized stub does not trigger loading the other fields from the database. Using the natural identifier also saves the overhead of artificial ID storage and generation, although this gain is often much smaller than imagined and can even be a net performance loss, particularly in cases where multiple columns make up the natural ID.

If the `natural` key is a single column, explicitly declare the `id` property and give it the appropriate type. Either approach will almost always require the ID generator to be set to `assigned`—otherwise Hibernate will attempt to assign a value to the `id` property, which will probably result in a type error.

Code Listing 2-10. Using an Individual Natural Identifier

```
// In ./grails-app/domain/Bar.groovy
class Bar {
  String id
  static mapping = {
    id generator:'assigned'
  }
}
```

Sometimes more than one value is required for the natural identifier. This kind of database identifier is called a "composite" identifier. To use a composite natural ID instead of an artificial ID, use the `composite` key on the `id` call in the mapping DSL. The value of that key is a list of the natural

ID field names. Additionally, due to surprising consequences upstream in Hibernate, the domain object itself needs to implement the `Serializable` interface (for more on this see the section on `get` in Chapter 3).

Code Listing 2-11. Using a Composite Natural Identifier

```
// In ./grails-app/domain/Foo.groovy
class Foo implements Serializable {
  String code1, code2
  static mapping = {
    id composite:[code1, code2]
  }
}
```

Customizing Relationship Links

In a normal one-to-many relationship, the foreign key link is stored on the child's table. Using the mapping DSL you can alter the name of this link by setting the `column` key on the parent's association entry.

If the one-to-many relationship is prone to becoming a many-to-many relationship in the future, the one-to-many relationship can be coerced into using a join table from the start. To do this, the parent's association entry is passed the `joinTable` key, the value of which is a map specifying `name`, `key` (i.e. the parent's foreign key), and `column` (i.e. the child's foreign key).

For a many-to-many relationship, each side of the relationship is responsible for its own foreign key information, which is specified on the mapping DSL using the `column` key on the association entry. One bit of awkwardness comes when changing the join table: the new join table name needs to be specified the same way on both sides of the relationship, or there will be a data inconsistency as a result.

```groovy
// In ./grails-app/domain/Foo.groovy
class Foo {
  static hasMany = [
    bar:Bar,     // one-to-many
    bazzes:Baz,  // one-to-many (join table)
    junks:Junk   // many-to-many
  ]
  static mapping = {
    bars column:'FK_Foo_Id'
    bazzes joinTable:[
            name:'Foo_Baz_Link',
            key: 'Foo_Id_Key',
            column: 'Baz_Id_Column'
    ]
    junks column:'Foo_FK', joinTable:'foojunks'
  }
}


// In ./grails-app/domain/Junk.groovy
class Junk {
  static hasMany = [foos:Foo]
  static belongsTo = Foo
  static mapping = {
    foos column:'Junk_FK', joinTable:'foojunks'
  }
}


// In ./grails-app/domain/Bar.groovy
class Bar {
```

```
  static belongsTo = [foo:Foo]
}


// In ./grails-app/domain/Baz.groovy
class Baz {
  static belongsTo = [foo:Foo]
}
```

Custom Association Fetching Strategies

By default, Hibernate's lazy evaluation results in a single query, plus a
single query for each collection when that collection is encountered, plus a
single query for each domain object property when that domain object
property is encountered. This structure works well for the common case of
web development, when a reasonably small subset of each domain object is
actually accessed in a given session.

Sometimes, however, there are aspects of the domain that will make such a
lazy load less well-performing than the alternatives. In particular, if you
have a domain object with an association that is almost always going to be
loaded, it may be valuable to set the fields to load eagerly. Similarly,
rarely-used or very large domain object properties may be better off loaded
lazily. Both of these cases are handled by using the lazy key, which takes
a Boolean value.

Note   There is also a fetchMode property, but the mapping ORM
behavior will override it. Do not mix and match these properties or you will
confuse yourself.

Code Listing 2-13. Customizing Lazy Fetching Example

```
// In ./grails-app/domain/Foo.groovy
class Foo {
  static hasMany = [ bars:Bar ]
  Baz baz
  static mapping = {
    baz lazy:true
    bars lazy:false
  }
}
```

The Second-Level Cache

One of the most valuable tools of Hibernate is its intermediary cache with the database. The Hibernate session itself acts as a cache that consolidates repeated `save` calls and prevents fetches on the same object.[6] The second-level cache can be thought of as an extension of that capability: it caches objects at an additional intermediary level between the session caches and the database itself. This can result in a substantial speed increase for often-used data, but at some slight risk. If the data is modified in the database outside of GORM, stale data may be retrieved by GORM. In many cases this risk is very acceptable, particularly when data is read-only or write-rarely.

By default, the second-level cache is used only for query results and uses OpenSymphony's OSCache as an implementation. These values can be altered in `./grails-app/conf/DataSource.groovy` by adjusting the `hibernate` properties found there.

---

[6] Some examples of this book *want* repeated object fetches, and hence the explicit calls to `sessionFactory.currentSession.clear()`.

Object Cache

An entire domain object class may be eligible for caching by placing `cache true` in the mapping DSL. In this case all the class's properties are stored in the second-level cache when they are read from the database. When an update or delete is applied to the data the item is evicted from the cache and refreshed on the next read. This is called a `read-write` cache.

This behavior can be further customized using the `usage` and `include` keys for the `cache` call. The `usage` key specifies whether to use `read-only` or `read-write` caching. The `read-only` usage is substantially faster than the default `read-write` usage but has no capability of safely handling updates to domain objects. There are other potential settings for the `usage` key; however, they are not appropriate for the Grails context. The `include` key can be specified as `non-lazy` in order to cache only those properties that are not lazily fetched. This setting is very useful for keeping large, rarely-accessed properties from bloating your cache.

Code Listing 2-14. Enabling Object Cache for a Class

```
// In ./grails-app/domain/Foo.groovy
class Foo {
  static mapping = {
    cache true
  }
}
// In ./grails-app/domain/Bar.groovy
class Bar {
  static mapping = {
    cache usage:'read-only', include:'non-lazy'
  }
}
```

Association Caching

The association cache is arguably the more valuable part of the second-level cache. The association cache is responsible for caching the collection of objects associated with a given domain class, which is often the most painful part of domain object retrieval.

To enable association caching of the second-level class, specify the `cache` key on the association call of the mapping DSL. If the value is set to `true` or `'read-write'`, a read-write cache is used for the associations. If the associations do not change, a `'read-only'` value can be passed in to use the more efficient read-only cache. If the `'read-only'` cache is used an exception will be thrown from any attempt to write to the collection, which makes it valuable only for pre-loaded collection data.

Code Listing 2-15. Enabling an Association Cache

```
// In ./grails-app/domain/Foo.groovy
class Foo {
  static hasMany = [bars:Bar]
  static mapping = {
    bars cache:'read-write'
  }
}
```

Mapping Inheritance and Table-Per-Subclass Inheritance

As explored in "Creating and Defining Inheritance Trees" in Chapter 1, GORM's default behavior is to create a single table that stores the data for the entire inheritance tree; this is referred to as the table-per-hierarchy approach. While this works fine for small structures, larger trees or trees that include BLOB or CLOB objects simply become unwieldy.

In this case the better approach is table-per-subclass, which creates a distinct table for each subclass and performs the appropriate inner joins up the hierarchy chain to retrieve data. Performance is often much worse but it is both theoretically cleaner and can beat out the table-per-hierarchy approach in rare boundary cases. To adopt the table-per-subclass approach, specify `tablePerHierarchy false` in the root class's mapping DSL.

Disabling Optimistic Locking

To disable optimistic locking simply pass `false` to `version` in the mapping DSL. This saves a database column, but the domain object needs to be locked at the database level when it is going to be updated. In general, the cost of optimistic locking is so small that it should be left in play as a safeguard, even if it is seemingly redundant with pessimistic locking practices. For read-only domain objects, however, the optimistic locking can be disabled without consequence.

Demystifying Cascades

When a save or delete happens on one domain object, that save or delete may trigger saves or deletes on other objects. This behavior is referred to as a **cascade** and is meant as a convenience for the user. Undoubtedly the most error-prone part of learning GORM, though, is understanding how cascades impact the database.

The first thing to remember is that saves always cascade down, but `belongsTo` acts a bridge allowing deletes to cascade down relationships.

```groovy
// In ./grails-app/domain/Foo.groovy
class Foo {
  static hasMany = [bars:Bar, bazzes:Baz]
}
// In ./grails-app/domain/Bar.groovy
class Bar {
  static belongsTo = [foo:Foo]
}
// In ./grails-app/domain/Baz.groovy
class Baz {
  // Does not belongTo Foo
}
// In ./test/integration/FooTests.groovy
  void testCascadingSaveAndDelete() {
    def foo = new Foo(bars:[], bazzes:[])
    def bar = new Bar()
    def baz = new Baz()
    foo.addToBars(bar)
    foo.addToBazzes(baz)
    assertNotNull foo.save()
    assertNotNull foo.id
    assertNotNull bar.id // Cascading save
    assertNotNull baz.id // Cascading save
    foo.delete()
    assertNull Bar.get(bar.id) // Cascading delete
    assertNotNull Baz.get(baz.id) // Not deleted
  }
```

Although not often done, if one class specifies that it belongsTo another without its parent class knowing about it, there is no cascading behavior in either direction. Note that this is in direct conflict with the documentation as of this writing.

Code Listing 2-17. Demonstrating Unpaired `belongsTo`

```
// In ./grails-app/domain/Foo.groovy
class Foo {
}
// In ./grails-app/domain/Junk.groovy
class Junk {
  static belongsTo = [foo:Foo]
}
// In ./test/integration/FooTests.groovy
  void testUnidirectionalParentDelete() {
    def foo = new Foo()
    assertNotNull foo.save() // No cascading save
    def junk = new Junk(foo:foo)
    assertNotNull junk.save()
    foo.delete(flush:true)
    sessionFactory.currentSession.clear()
    assertNotNull Junk.get(junk.id)
    shouldFail {
      Foo.get(foo.id)
    }
  }
```

Chapter 3: Querying with GORM and HQL

"The art and science of asking questions is the source of all knowledge."

Thomas Berger

When developing a project, whether iteratively or otherwise, defining the model is a critical and significant piece of work. However, the real advantage of GORM over vanilla Hibernate is in the powerful and extensive set of querying methods. GORM automatically injects methods onto the domain classes which address most of the common querying scenarios, including querying the GORM domain by ID or properties.

For those used to more complex application architectures, think of GORM as providing a data access object (DAO) hanging right off of the domain class itself, already preconfigured with most of the methods you will use.

For everyone else, think of GORM as providing prewritten methods and other tools to save you a whole lot of SQL writing. These tools include a very useful and impressive domain object querying DSL called the Hibernate Query Language (HQL).

Querying via Direct Methods on GORM Classes

get

The basic retrieval method in Grails, `get` is so simple it was actually slipped into unit tests earlier in the book. The `get` method takes the ID of a domain object to retrieve and returns the domain object with that ID. If no such domain object is found, it returns `null`.

Code Listing 3-1. Demonstrating get *in the Standard Case*

```
// In ./grails-app/domain/Foo.groovy
class Foo {}
// In ./test/integration/FooTests.groovy
  void testGet() {
    def foo = new Foo()
    assertNotNull foo.save()
    assertEquals foo, Foo.get(foo.id)
    assertNull Foo.get(foo.id * 9) // No exception
  }
```

If you have customized the id property to be a type other than the default, the get method will take the appropriate type and do the retrieval in the exact same way.

Code Listing 3-2. Demonstrating get *in the String ID Case*

```
// In ./grails-app/domain/Bar.groovy
class Bar {
  String id
  static mapping = {
    id generator:'assigned'
  }
}
// In ./test/integration/BarTests.groovy
  void testGetStringId() {
    def bar = new Bar()
    bar.id = 'bar'
    assertNotNull bar.save()
    assertEquals bar, Bar.get('bar')
  }
```

The only particularly tricky or surprising scenario involves domain classes with composite keys. To retrieve a domain object with that structure, use `get` on an instance of the domain class with the ID values populated.

Code Listing 3-3. Demonstrating `get` in the Composite ID Case

```
// In ./grails-app/domain/Foo.groovy
class Foo implements Serializable {
  String code1, code2, code3
  static mapping = {
    id composite:['code1', 'code2']
  }
}
// In ./test/integration/FooTests.groovy
  void testGetCompositeIds() {
    def foo = new Foo(
    code1:'klaatu',
    code2:'barada',
   code3:'nikto'
    )
    assertNotNull foo.save()
    assertEquals foo, Foo.get(new Foo(
    code1: 'klaatu',
   code2:'barada'
    ))
  }
```

getAll

The `getAll` method provides the same functionality as `get` except it retrieves a list of domain objects instead of just one. There are two forms of `getAll`: a varargs version and a list version, which means it can basically be called with a series of arguments (varargs) or with a list.

The ordering of the arguments is important. The returned list is a direct mapping of IDs onto objects; if an ID does not exist in the database the returned list will have `null` in the corresponding slot.

Tip   If you want to work only with non-null elements make the call something like `Foo.getAll(ids).findAll { it }` or the more Java-esque `def x = Foo.getAll(ids); x.removeAll(null)`.

Code Listing 3-4. Demonstrating `getAll`

```
// In ./grails-app/domain/Foo.groovy
class Foo {}
// In ./test/integration/FooTests.groovy
  void testGetAll() {
    def foos = []
    10.times { foos << new Foo() }
    foos*.save()
    def badFooId = foos*.id.max() + 1
    assertNull Foo.get(badFooId)
    def expected = foos[0..2]
    def actual = Foo.getAll([foos[0].id,
                             foos[1].id,
                       foos[2].id])
    assertEquals expected, actual
    expected = foos[0..3] + [null] + foos[4..-1]
    actual = Foo.getAll(foos[0..3]*.id + [badFooId] +
                       foos[4..-1]*.id)
    assertEquals expected, actual
  }
```

lock

Although optimistic locking is sufficient for most cases, a domain object will sometimes be altered, so it is important no other transaction tries to alter it at the same time. This kind of exclusive locking is called a **pessimistic lock**. A pessimistic lock can be accomplished by using `lock`. It behaves exactly the same as `get` but acquires the lock in addition to retrieving the value. The lock is released when the transaction is committed.

Caution   While the default database shipped with Grails, HSQLDB, works fairly well for development purposes, it has some significant limitations, one of which is that it does not support pessimistic locking.

---

list

The `list` method provides a way to retrieve a series of domain objects for a given class. The particular nature of the series is driven by named arguments: when given no arguments, it simply returns all the domain objects.

The `max/offset` parameters can be used to implement pagination. The series will return at most `max` elements, beginning at the zero-based `offset`. To implement pagination, the next page begins at the previous page's `max`, and the previous page's offset is the current `offset` - `max`. The properties can also be used independently of each other, should that ever be useful.

The `sort/order` parameters define the ordering of the returned elements. The `sort` parameter takes the property name to sort by and the `order` parameter is either `asc` (ascending) or `desc` (descending). By default, strings are sorted in a case-insensitive manner, but you can force a case-sensitive parameter by setting the `ignoreCase` parameter to `false`.

Caution　MySQL's default installation uses a collation that is not sensitive to case and GORM cannot override that configuration. To work around this problem, have your database administrator set your database default to `binary` collation. Or use Postgres.

The `fetch` parameter can be used to eagerly fetch relationships or properties that are normally lazily initialized. This parameter takes a map as an argument, where the keys are property names and the argument is `eager`.

Code Listing 3-5. Demonstrating `list`

```
// In ./grails-app/domain/Bar.groovy
class Bar { static belongsTo = [foo:Foo] }
// In ./grails-app/domain/Foo.groovy
class Foo {
  static hasMany = [bars:Bar]
  String name = ""
  static mapping = {
    bars lazy:true
  }
  String toString() { name }
}
// In ./test/integration/FooTests.groovy
  void testList() {
    def foos = []
    10.times { foos << new Foo() }
    foos*.save()
```

```
      assertTrue foos.containsAll(Foo.list())
      assertTrue Foo.list().containsAll(foos)
  }
  void testListPagination() {
    def foos = []
    9.times { foos << new Foo() }
    foos*.save()
    def page1 = [offset:0, max:3]
    def page2 = [offset:3, max:3]
    def page3 = [offset:6, max:3]
    def page4 = [offset:9, max:3]
    assertEquals 3, Foo.list(page1).size()
    assertEquals 3, Foo.list(page2).size()
    assertEquals 3, Foo.list(page3).size()
    assertEquals 0, Foo.list(page4).size()
    assertEquals([], Foo.list(page1).intersect(
                    Foo.list(page2)))
    assertEquals([], Foo.list(page2).intersect(
                    Foo.list(page3)))
    assertEquals([], Foo.list(page1).intersect(
                    Foo.list(page3)))
    def listAll = Foo.list(page1) +
                  Foo.list(page2) +
                  Foo.list(page3)
    assertTrue foos.containsAll(listAll)
    assertTrue listAll.containsAll(foos)
  }
  void testListSorting() {
    def foos = [:]
    ['bilbo', 'gimli', 'aragorn',
      'legolas', 'Frodo'].each {
```

```
      foos[it] = new Foo(name:it)
    }
    foos.values()*.save()
    assertEquals([
      foos.aragorn, foos.bilbo, foos.Frodo,
      foos.gimli, foos.legolas
    ], Foo.list(sort:'name'))
    assertEquals([
      foos.legolas, foos.gimli, foos.Frodo,
      foos.bilbo, foos.aragorn
    ], Foo.list(sort:'name', order:'desc'))

    assertEquals([
      foos.Frodo, foos.aragorn, foos.bilbo,
      foos.gimli, foos.legolas
    ], Foo.list(sort:'name', ignoreCase:false))
  }
  void testListFetching() {
    def foo = new Foo(name:'name')
    (1..<10).each {
      foo.addToBars(new Bar())
      //foo.addToBazzes(new Baz())
    }
    assertNotNull foo.save(flush:true)
    sessionFactory.currentSession.clear()
    foo = Foo.list()[0]
    assertFalse Hibernate.isInitialized(foo.bars)
    sessionFactory.currentSession.clear()
    foo = Foo.list(fetch:[bars:'eager'])[0]
    assertTrue Hibernate.isInitialized(foo.bars)
  }
```

listOrderBy*

The `list` method provides a `sort` argument to sort the elements by a particular property. That same behavior can be achieved by using the `listOrderBy*` family of methods. These methods take all the same arguments as `list`, but instead of using the `sort` argument the property to sort by is passed directly in the method name. The only semantic difference is that `String` properties are sorted in case-sensitive order by default using `listOrderBy*`.

Code Listing 3-6. Demonstrating `listOrderBy*`

```
// In ./grails-app/domain/Foo.groovy
class Foo { String name = "" }
// In ./test/integration/FooTests.groovy
  void testListOrderBySorting() {
    def foos = [:]
    ['bilbo', 'gimli', 'aragorn',
     'legolas', 'Frodo'].each {
      foos[it] = new Foo(name:it)
    }
    foos.values()*.save()
    assertEquals([
      foos.Frodo, foos.aragorn, foos.bilbo,
      foos.gimli, foos.legolas
    ], Foo.list(sort:'name', ignoreCase:false))
    assertEquals Foo.list(sort:'name',
ignoreCase:false),
                Foo.listOrderByName()
  }
```

findBy*/findAllBy*

findBy* and findAllBy* are the workhorse query methods in GORM. Both of them query the domain based on the name of the method. In the simplest approach, the property being queried on is specified in the method name and the value for that property is passed as an argument. The findBy* method will return one instance matching that value; the findAllBy* method will return all instances matching that value. The pagination parameters used for list (max, order, offset, and sort) may be used for findAllBy* to limit the number of results returned. Simply pass those parameters in the last argument as a map.

Caution The findBy* method will not error out if multiple potential matches exist in the domain. The particular instance returned is not specified.

Code Listing 3-7. Demonstrating findBy* *and* findAllBy* *(Simple)*

```
// In ./grails-app/domain/Foo.groovy
class Foo { String name = "" }
// In ./test/integration/FooTests.groovy
  void testFindBy() {
    def foo = new Foo(name:'Smokejumper')
    assertNotNull foo.save()
    assertEquals foo, Foo.findByName('Smokejumper')
  }
  void testFindByWithDuplicates() {
    (1..2).each {
      assertNotNull new Foo(name:'Smokejumper').save()
    }
    assertNotNull Foo.findByName('Smokejumper')
```

```
  }
  void testFindAllBy() {
    def foos = [] as Set
    (1..2).each {
      foos << new Foo(name:'Smokejumper')
    }
    foos*.save()
    assertEquals foos,
                 Foo.findAllByName('Smokejumper') as Set
  }
```

Conjunctions (and/or)

This family of methods is even more advanced than that, though. Multiple properties can be queried by using And and Or. Only one conjunction is allowed per method, and this is an explicit design decision—there are other ways to do more complicated queries.

Code Listing 3-8. Conjoined `findBy*`/`findAllBy*`

```
// In ./grails-app/domain/Foo.groovy
class Foo {
  String name = ""
  int rank = 0
}
// In ./test/integration/FooTests.groovy
void testFindByAndFindAllByWithAnd() {
  assertNotNull new Foo(name:'Smokejumper',
                        rank:2).save()
  assertNotNull Foo.findByNameAndRank('Smokejumper', 2)
  assertEquals 1,
Foo.findAllByNameAndRank('Smokejumper',
                                    2).size()
```

```
  }
  void testFindByAndFindAllByWithOr() {
    assertNotNull new Foo(name:'Smokejumper',
                          rank:2).save()
    assertNotNull new Foo(name:'Robert', rank:1).save()
    assertNotNull Foo.findByNameOrRank('Unused', 2)
    assertNotNull Foo.findByNameOrRank('Robert', 3)
    assertEquals 2, Foo.findAllByNameOrRank('Robert',
                                            2).size()
    assertEquals 1, Foo.findAllByNameOrRank('Robert',
                                            1).size()
  }
```

Operators

The power of these methods still does not stop there. It is even possible to incorporate some minor logic into the method name, such as these operators:

Range Operators: `LessThan`, `LessThanEquals`, `GreaterThan`, `GreaterThanEquals`, `Between`, `NotEqual`

String Operators: `Like`, `Ilike`

Null Operators: `IsNull`, `IsNotNull`

Caution   The range operators, including `NotEqual`, will never return an instance whose property is `null`. Also note that there is no `Equal`, despite what the Grails documentation may say: leaving the operator off handles that case.

Code Listing 3-9. Demonstrating `list` **with** *Operators*

```groovy
// In ./grails-app/domain/Foo.groovy
class Foo {
  String name = ""
  int rank = 0
  static constraints = {
    name(nullable:true)
  }
  String toString() { "$name $rank" }
}
// In ./test/integration/FooTests.groovy
  void testOperators() {
    def foo1 = new Foo(name:'foo', rank:1).save()
    def foo2 = new Foo(name:'foo', rank:2).save()
    def foo3 = new Foo(name:'Foo', rank:3).save()
    def fob0 = new Foo(name:'fob', rank:0).save()
    def bar1 = new Foo(name:'bar', rank:1).save()
    def null4 = new Foo(name:null, rank:4).save()
    assertEquals([foo1,foo2,foo3,fob0,bar1] as Set
      Foo.findAllByRankLessThan(4) as Set)
    assertEquals([foo1,bar1,fob0] as Set,
      Foo.findAllByRankLessThanEquals(1) as Set)
    assertEquals([foo3,null4] as Set,
      Foo.findAllByRankGreaterThan(2) as Set)
    assertEquals([foo2,foo3,null4] as Set,
      Foo.findAllByRankGreaterThanEquals(2) as Set)
    assertEquals([foo2, foo3] as Set,
      Foo.findAllByRankBetween(2,3) as Set)
    assertEquals([foo1,foo2,fob0] as Set,
      Foo.findAllByNameLike('fo%') as Set)
```

```
        assertEquals([foo1,foo2,foo3,fob0] as Set,
           Foo.findAllByNameIlike('fo%') as Set)
        assertEquals([foo1,foo2,foo3,fob0,bar1] as Set,
           Foo.findAllByNameIsNotNull() as Set)
        assertEquals([null4], Foo.findAllByNameIsNull())
        assertEquals([foo3, fob0, bar1], // null4 not found
           Foo.findAllByNameNotEqual('foo'))
    }
```

Querying for Embedded Fields and Has-One Relationships

To query for embedded fields and has-one relationships, use an example
instance to specify the field you are looking up. For an embedded field this
value has to be fully populated; for a has-one relationship, the ID field
needs to be specified.

Code Listing 3-10. Demonstrating `findBy` *on Embedded Fields and
Has-One Relationships*

```
// In ./src/groovy/Name.groovy
class Name { String first, last }
// In ./grails-app/domain/Baz.groovy
class Baz { static belongsTo = [foo:Foo] }
// In ./grails-app/domain/Foo.groovy
class Foo {
  static embedded = ['name']
  Baz baz = new Baz()
  Name name = new Name(first:'', last:'')
}
// In ./test/integration/FooTests.groovy
  void testFindByEmbeddedField() {
    def name = new Name(first:'Robert', last:'Fischer')
    def foo = new Foo(name:name).save()
```

```
    assertNotNull foo
    name = new Name(first:'Robert', last:'Fischer')
    assertNotNull Foo.findByName(name)
    name = new Name(first:'Robert')
    assertNull Foo.findByName(name)
  }
  void testFindByOnHasOneRelationship() {
    def baz = new Baz()
    def foo = new Foo(baz:baz)
    assertNotNull foo.save()
    assertNotNull Foo.findByBaz(baz)
  }
```

Querying via the Criteria Builder

If a query becomes more complicated than findAllBy* or findBy* can
support, one option is to use an embedded DSL called the Criteria Builder.
The Criteria Builder extends the Hibernate Criteria API[7] with a more tree-
like syntax. The power of this structure is the ability to integrate arbitrary
Groovy code, including control structures, loops, and method calls, into the
generation of a query. Often ORM frameworks have overlooked or
downplayed the value of integrating program logic with database access,
but this is actually an area where GORM excels.

There are two access points from a GORM domain class into the Criteria
Builder. The succinct, inline version of the Criteria Builder's "list"
functionality is invoked via withCriteria; a Criteria Builder as an object
can be retrieved by using createCriteria.

---

[7] http://hibernate.org/hib_docs/v3/reference/en/
html/querycriteria.html

Code Listing 3-11. Comparing `withCriteria/createCriteria/list`

```
// In ./grails-app/domain/Foo.groovy
class Foo {}
// In ./test/integration/FooTests.groovy
  void testListEquivalency() {
    (1..10).each {
      assertNotNull new Foo().save()
    }
    assertEquals 10, Foo.list().size()
    assertEquals Foo.list(), Foo.withCriteria {}
    assertEquals Foo.list(), Foo.createCriteria().list
{}
  }
```

Querying Properties

To query a property value, use one of the comparison operators, which. These are called like methods within the criteria block. The comparison operators are as follows:

Equality/Range Value Operators: between, eq, gt, ge, idEq, 'in',[8] lt, ne

Equality/Range Property Operators: eqProperty, gtProperty, geProperty, ltProperty, neProperty (these compare two properties to one another on the database itself)

Null Operators: isNull, isNotNull

String Operators: ilike, like

---

[8] Because in is a Groovy keyword it has to be set in single quotes. It looks funny, but Groovy will resolve the quoted string to be a dynamic method call as long as it is followed with a left parenthesis.

Note   The properties being queried must be directly on the object and cannot be artificial properties or GPath expressions. The only apparent exception to this is for embedded properties, which are resolved in a GPath-like expression (see the test named `testOperatorOnEmbedded` in Code Listing 3-12).

Code Listing 3-12. Querying Properties with Criteria Builder

```
// In ./src/groovy/Name.groovy
class Name { String first, last }
// In ./grails-app/domain/Foo.groovy
class Foo {
  static embedded = ['name']
  String code1 = ''
  String code2 = ''
  Name name = new Name(first:'', last:'')
  static constraints = {
    code2(nullable:true)
  }
}
// In ./test/integration/FooTests.groovy
void testEqualityRangeValueOperators() {
  def fooA = new Foo(code1:'A')
  assertNotNull fooA.save()
  def fooB = new Foo(code1:'B')
  assertNotNull fooB.save()
  def fooC = new Foo(code1:'C')
  assertNotNull fooC.save()
  assertEquals([fooB,fooC] as Set,
    Foo.withCriteria {
      between('code1', 'B', 'C')
```

```
    } as Set)
  assertEquals([fooA] as Set,
    Foo.withCriteria { eq('code1', 'A') } as Set)
  assertEquals([fooC] as Set,
    Foo.withCriteria { gt('code1', 'B') } as Set)
  assertEquals([fooB, fooC] as Set,
    Foo.withCriteria { ge('code1', 'B') } as Set)
  assertEquals([fooA] as Set,
    Foo.withCriteria { idEq(fooA.id) } as Set)
  assertEquals([fooA,fooB] as Set,
     Foo.withCriteria {
        'in'('code1', ['A','B'])
     } as Set)
  assertEquals([fooA] as Set,
    Foo.withCriteria { lt('code1', 'B') } as Set)
  assertEquals([fooA, fooB] as Set,
    Foo.withCriteria { le('code1', 'B') } as Set)
  assertEquals([fooA, fooC] as Set,
    Foo.withCriteria { ne('code1', 'B') } as Set)
}
void testEqualityRangePropertyOperators() {
  def fooA = new Foo(code1:'A', code2:'A')
  assertNotNull fooA.save()
  def fooB = new Foo(code1:'A', code2:'B')
  assertNotNull fooB.save()
  assertEquals([fooA] as Set,
    Foo.withCriteria {
      eqProperty('code1','code2')
    } as Set)
  assertEquals([fooB] as Set,
    Foo.withCriteria {
```

```
      gtProperty('code2','code1')
    } as Set)
  assertEquals([fooA, fooB] as Set,
    Foo.withCriteria {
      geProperty('code2','code1')
    } as Set)
  assertEquals([fooB] as Set,
    Foo.withCriteria {
      ltProperty('code1','code2')
    } as Set)
  assertEquals([fooA, fooB] as Set,
    Foo.withCriteria {
      leProperty('code1','code2')
    } as Set)
  assertEquals([fooB] as Set,
    Foo.withCriteria {
      neProperty('code1','code2')
    } as Set)
}
void testNullOperators() {
  def fooWith2 = new Foo(code1:'A', code2:'B')
  assertNotNull fooWith2.save()
  def fooNo2 = new Foo(code1:'A', code2:null)
  assertNotNull fooNo2.save()
  assertEquals([fooNo2] as Set,
    Foo.withCriteria { isNull('code2') } as Set)
  assertEquals([fooWith2] as Set,
    Foo.withCriteria { isNotNull('code2') } as Set)
}
void testStringOperators() {
  def caffoo = new Foo(code1:'caffoo')
```

```
    assertNotNull caffoo.save()
    def food = new Foo(code1:'food')
    assertNotNull food.save()
    def foo = new Foo(code1:'foo')
    assertNotNull foo.save()
    def bigFoo = new Foo(code1:'FOO')
    assertNotNull bigFoo.save()
    assertEquals([caffoo, foo] as Set,
      Foo.withCriteria { like('code1', '%foo') } as Set)
    assertEquals([caffoo, foo, food] as Set,
      Foo.withCriteria { like('code1', '%foo%') } as Set)
    assertEquals([caffoo, foo, food, bigFoo] as Set,
      Foo.withCriteria { ilike('code1', '%foo%') } as Set)
  }
  void testOperatorOnEmbedded() {
    def name = new Name(first:'Robert', last:'Fischer')
    def foo = new Foo(code1:'A', name:name)
    assertNotNull foo.save()
    assertEquals([foo] as Set,
      Foo.withCriteria { eq('name', name) } as Set)
  }
```

Conjunctions (and/or)

Properties can be joined by using the and and or operators. Both operators take a block and sibling builder calls inside that block are logically combined.

Code Listing 3-13. Demonstrating and *and* or *in Criteria Builder*

```
// In ./grails-app/domain/Foo.groovy
class Foo { String code1 = '', code2 = '' }
// In ./test/integration/FooTests.groovy
  void testAndOr() {
    def fooAA = new Foo(code1:'A', code2:'A')
    assertNotNull fooAA.save()
    def fooAB = new Foo(code1:'A', code2:'B')
    assertNotNull fooAB.save()
    assertEquals([fooAB] as Set,
      Foo.withCriteria {
        and {
          eq('code1', 'A')
          eq('code2', 'B')
        }
      } as Set)
    assertEquals([fooAA, fooAB] as Set,
      Foo.withCriteria {
        or {
          eq('code1', 'A')
          eq('code2', 'B')
        }
      } as Set)
  }
```

The and conjunction in the previous example is a bit redundant. The default behavior for nonspecified sibling calls is to and them together.

Code Listing 3-14. Proving Default Builder Conjunction Is and

```
void testDefaultIsAnd() {
    def foo = new Foo(code1:'Frodo', code2:'Baggins')
    assertNotNull foo.save()
    def withAnd = Foo.withCriteria {
                    and {
                        eq('code1','Frodo')
                        eq('code2','Baggins')
                    }
                }
    assertEquals([foo], withAnd)
    assertEquals(withAnd, Foo.withCriteria {
                        eq('code1','Frodo')
                        eq('code2','Baggins')
                    })
}
```

Negation (not)

The not operator takes a block like and and or but requires that its child
checks fail.

Code Listing 3-15. Demonstrating not in Criteria Builder

```
// In ./grails-app/domain/Foo.groovy
class Foo { String code1 = '', code2 = '' }
// In ./test/integration/FooTests.groovy
  void testNot() {
    def fooCA = new Foo(code1:'C', code2:'A')
    assertNotNull fooCA.save()
    def fooDB = new Foo(code1:'D', code2:'B')
    assertNotNull fooDB.save()
```

```
    assertEquals([fooCA] as Set,
      Foo.withCriteria {
        not {
          eq('code2', 'B')
        }
      } as Set)
  }
```

Paginated Results (`maxResults`/`firstResult`/`order`)

The builder provides a simple way to structure pagination: three methods called `maxResults`, `firstResult`, and `order`. `maxResult` takes an argument of the maximum number of results to return; `firstResult` takes an argument of the offset into the results (zero-based); and `order` takes an argument of the parameter to order by and optionally the direction to sort—`asc` or `desc`.

Code Listing 3-16. Demonstrating Pagination with Criteria Builder

```
// In ./grails-app/domain/Foo.groovy
class Foo { int code }
// In ./test/integration/FooTests.groovy
  void testPagination() {
    (1..10).each {
      assertNotNull new Foo(code:it).save()
    }
    assertEquals([1,2,3], Foo.withCriteria {
      maxResults(3)
      firstResult(0)
      order('code','asc')
    }*.code)
    assertEquals([9,10], Foo.withCriteria {
      maxResults(3)
```

```
      firstResult(8)
      order('code')
    }*.code)
  }
```

Querying Relationships

Although Criteria Builder's capabilities are useful enough when acting on just a single domain class, its relationship query structures are truly impressive. By leveraging a tree-like structure, the builder gives a succinct syntax to what would be complicated join logic and awkward aliasing in SQL/HQL. In most cases the builder provides the cleanest and most maintainable way to express relationship-traversing queries.

To build a relationship into part of the query, simply call the relationship name with a closure. The closure provides a place to specify the requirements on that relationship. If any value in a has-many relationship matches the requirements, the requirement will pass.

Code Listing 3-17. Demonstrating Criteria Builder Relationships

```
// In ./grails-app/domain/Foo.groovy
class Foo {
  static hasMany = [bars:Bar]
  int code
}
// In ./grails-app/domain/Bar.groovy
class Bar {
  static belongsTo = [foo:Foo]
  int value
}
// In ./test/integration/FooTests.groovy
  void testRelationshipExample() {
    def goodBar = new Bar(value:2)
```

```
def goodFoo = new Foo(code:1)
goodFoo.addToBars(goodBar)
assertNotNull goodFoo.save()
def badBar = new Bar(value:3)
def badFoo = new Foo(code:1)
badFoo.addToBars(badBar)
assertNotNull badFoo.save()
assertEquals([goodFoo], Foo.withCriteria {
  eq('code',1)
  bars {
    eq('value',2)
  }
})
}
```

Relationship Size Operators (`isEmpty`/`isNotEmpty`/`sizeEq`)

In addition to the basic operators, a has-many relationship can be queried for its size. This is particularly useful in pre-filtering parent instances when children are being processed.

These relationship operators are treated like property operators: instead of creating a tree for the property, simply call them on the parent and pass in the relationship property name.

Code Listing 3-18. Demonstrating Relationship Size Operators

```
// In ./test/integration/FooTests.groovy
  void testRelationshipSizes() {
    def fooWith0 = new Foo(code:0)
    assertNotNull fooWith0.save()
    def fooWith1 = new Foo(code:1)
    fooWith1.addToBars(new Bar(value:1))
    assertNotNull fooWith1.save()
```

```
    assertEquals 1, fooWith1.bars.size()
    def fooWith2 = new Foo(code:2)
    (1..2).each {
      fooWith2.addToBars(new Bar(value:it))
    }
    assertNotNull fooWith2.save()
    assertEquals 2, fooWith2.bars.size()
    assertEquals([fooWith0], Foo.withCriteria {
      isEmpty('bars')
    })
    assertEquals([fooWith1,fooWith2],
      Foo.withCriteria {
        isNotEmpty('bars')
      })
    assertEquals([fooWith1], Foo.withCriteria {
      sizeEq('bars',1)
    })
  }
```

Setting the Fetch Mode (fetchMode)

One common point of awkwardness is the way in which relationships are
fetched. At the point of querying the object, additional information is often
known about how to optimize the fetching, and appropriate. The
fetchMode method can be used to configure the pre-fetching behavior for
the query by passing it two arguments: the property of the collection to
configure, and the org.hibernate.FetchMode that is intended to be
loaded.

Following are the fetchMode options:

DEFAULT: Use the underlying mapping configuration.

JOIN: Use an outer join to fetch the relationship. This is the only explicit eager fetching mode and should be used when you know that all the objects in the collection will be touched.

SELECT: Use a distinct select to fetch the relationship when required. This is the only explicit lazy fetching mode. Lazy fetching should be preferred when there is a good chance most of the objects will not be used.

Code Listing 3-19. Demonstrating the `fetchMode` *Parameters*

```
void testRelationshipSizes() {
  def fooWith2 = new Foo(code:2)
  (1..2).each {
    fooWith2.addToBars(new Bar(value:it))
  }
  assertNotNull fooWith2.save()
  assertEquals 2, fooWith2.bars.size()
  sessionFactory.currentSession.clear()
  fooWith2 = Foo.get(fooWith2.id)
  assertFalse Hibernate.isInitialized(fooWith2.bars)
  sessionFactory.currentSession.clear()
  fooWith2 = Foo.withCriteria {
    fetchMode('bars', FetchMode.JOIN) // Outer join
  }[0]
  assertTrue Hibernate.isInitialized(fooWith2.bars)
  sessionFactory.currentSession.clear()
  fooWith2 = Foo.withCriteria {
    fetchMode('bars', FetchMode.SELECT) // Lazy fetch
  }[0]
  assertFalse Hibernate.isInitialized(fooWith2.bars)
  sessionFactory.currentSession.clear()
  fooWith2 = Foo.withCriteria {
    fetchMode('bars', FetchMode.DEFAULT) // Default
  }[0]
```

```
    assertFalse Hibernate.isInitialized(fooWith2.bars)
    sessionFactory.currentSession.clear()
}
```

Caution   Donald Knuth once quipped, "Premature optimization is the root of all evil." That quote should be kept as a guide in this area: the temptation to tweak is often more powerful than wise here. Because Hibernate has quite a few tricks and quite a bit of intelligence in fetching relationships and caching domain instances, overriding `fetchMode` will often not realize the gains a developer might expect.

Querying for Limited Data and Summaries (projections)

One goal when designing an ORM-based domain is to isolate small atoms of information to ensure information that is always used together is retrieved at once, but a minimum of additional information is brought along. By doing this the database can more accurately analyze and optimize its work, and lazy fetching has lots of opportunities to minimize the amount of data coming back from the database.

Even under that approach, information sometimes needs to be summarized from many, many records across the entire domain. In this case the powerful set of optimizations provided by Hibernate may not enough, and the heavy lifting for generating this report may need to be done in the database itself. The builder has the ability to generate this kind of information, and that capability is called **projections**.

Basic Projection Usage

To create a projection, call the `projections` method and pass it a closure. The closure can call any method from `org.hibernate.criterion.Projections`, but the simplest use is to call the `property` method to specify properties. When a single property is specified, the call returns a list of that property's values. When multiple properties are specified, the call returns a list of `Object` arrays containing the values of the properties.

Code Listing 3-20. Demonstrating Basic Projection Usage

```
// In ./grails-app/domain/Foo.groovy
class Foo { int code1, code2 }
// In ./test/integration/FooTests.groovy
  void testProjections() {
    [[42,23], [-1,-2], [-1,-2]].each {
      assertNotNull(new Foo(code1:it[0],
                            code2:it[1]).save())
    }
    def list = Foo.withCriteria {
      projections { property('code1') }
    }
    assertTrue list instanceof List
    assertEquals([-1,-1,42] as SortedSet,
                 list as SortedSet)
    def multilist = Foo.withCriteria {
      projections {
        property('code1')
        property('code2')
      }
    }
    assertTrue multilist instanceof List
    assertTrue multilist[0].class.isArray()
```

```
    assertEquals 42, multilist[0][0]
    assertEquals 23, multilist[0][1]
    assertEquals(-1, multilist[1][0])
    assertEquals(-2, multilist[1][1])
    assertEquals(-1, multilist[2][0])
    assertEquals(-2, multilist[2][1])
  }
```

Getting Unique Results (distinct)

A unique set of values from properties can be found via the distinct projection. Simply call the distinct projection with the column whose distinct values are desired. Multiple columns may be specified by calling distinct multiple times.

Code Listing 3-21. Demonstrating Getting Unique Results

```
    void testDistinct() {
      [[42,23], [-1,-2], [-1,-2]].each {
        assertNotNull(new Foo(code1:it[0],
                              code2:it[1]).save())
      }
      assertEquals([42,-1] as Set, Foo.withCriteria {
        projections { distinct('code1') }
      } as Set)
    }
```

Counting (count/rowCount/countDistinct)

Following are the three ways to get a count back in a projections block:

count: The count of rows based on a property, including null elements. Takes the property name as an argument.

rowCount: The equivalent of SQL's count(*), this returns the count of the number of rows. Takes no argument.

countDistinct: Returns the number of distinct values that the property has. Takes the property name as an argument.

Code Listing 3-22. Demonstrating `counts`

```
// In ./grails-app/domain/Foo.groovy
class Foo {
  int code1, code2
  static constraints = { code2(nullable:true) }
}
// In ./test/integration/FooTests.groovy
  void testCounts() {
    [[42,23], [-1,-2], [-1,null]].each {
      assertNotNull(new Foo(code1:it[0],
                            code2:it[1]).save())
    }
    assertEquals([2], Foo.withCriteria {
      projections { countDistinct('code1') }
    })
    assertEquals([3], Foo.withCriteria {
      projections { count('code2') }
    })
    assertEquals([3], Foo.withCriteria {
      projections { rowCount() }
    })
  }
```

Mathematical Summaries (`avg/max/min/sum`)

Rudimentary statistics are available within the `projections` block, as well. In particular, `avg`, `max`, `min`, and `sum` are available, each providing exactly the thing they are named. In the case of `avg`, the mean is provided.

It is somewhat tricky to remember, but the results are wrapped in a list even when only one value is requested.

Code Listing 3-23. Demonstrating Mathematical Summaries

```
void testMathematicalSummaries() {
  [[42,23], [-1,-2], [-1,-2]].each {
    assertNotNull(new Foo(code1:it[0],
                          code2:it[1]).save())
  }
  assertEquals([-1], Foo.withCriteria {
    projections { min('code1') }
  })
  assertEquals([42], Foo.withCriteria {
    projections { max('code1') }
  })
  assertEquals([42+-1+-1] as Set, Foo.withCriteria {
    projections { sum('code1') }
  } as Set)
  assertEquals([13.0d] as Set, Foo.withCriteria {
    projections { avg('code1') }
  } as Set)
}
```

Grouping (groupProperty)

Projections allow records to be grouped by property values. This is primarily useful in conjunction with the mathematical summaries or rowCount. To use grouping, call the groupProperty method inside projections and give it the name of the property to be grouped by. Multiple properties may be specified by calling groupProperty multiple times.

Code Listing 3-24. Demonstrating Grouping Using Projections

```
void testGroupProperty() {
  [[42,23], [-1,-2], [-1,2]].each {
    assertNotNull(new Foo(code1:it[0],
                          code2:it[1]).save())
  }
  def result = Foo.withCriteria {
    projections {
      groupProperty('code1')
      max('code2')
      rowCount()
    }
  }
  assertEquals([42, 23, 1], result[0] as List)
  assertEquals([-1, 2,  2], result[1] as List)
}
```

Explicit Methods (`list`/`listDistinct`/`get`/`scroll`)

Throughout the preceding examples, the Hibernate Criteria Builder has been accessed via a `withCriteria` call. There is also a `createCriteria` call that provides the criteria object itself. With that object it is possible to call methods that provide behaviors other than `list`, which simply lists the results. Although Hibernate usually handles this for you, occasionally joins result in nondistinct rows being returned, and then the `listDistinct` method may be called to guaranty uniqueness of the results. However, it is important to know that the `listDistinct` method will *not* guaranty the unique results in a projection. If only a single value is going to be returned, the `get` method may be called to return a single unboxed value. Finally, more traditional `ResultSet`-style scrollable results may be accessed by calling `scroll` and then navigating with `first()`, `next()`, `scroll(int)`, previous(), and last(). When the appropriate row is found, the value can be returned by calling get().

Code Listing 3-25. Demonstrating Explicit Retrieval Methods

```
void testListListDistinctGetScroll() {
  def foo42 = new Foo(code1:42, code2:23).save()
  [[1,2], [-1,-2]].each {
    assertNotNull(new Foo(code1:it[0],
                          code2:it[1]).save())
  }
  assertEquals(Foo.withCriteria {},
               Foo.createCriteria().list {})
  assertEquals(foo42, Foo.createCriteria().get {
    idEq(foo42.id)
  })
  def scroller = Foo.createCriteria().scroll {
    order('code1', 'desc')
  }
  assertTrue scroller.first() // Has first result
  assertEquals foo42, scroller.get()
  assertTrue scroller.next()
  assertEquals([1], scroller.get().code1)
  assertTrue scroller.first()
  assertTrue scroller.last()
  assertEquals([-1], scroller.get().code1)
  assertTrue scroller.previous()
  assertEquals([1], scroller.get().code1)
  assertTrue scroller.first()
  assertTrue scroller.scroll(2) // Move forward 2
  assertEquals([-1], scroller.get().code1)
}
```

Caution   Do not use `++` or `--` on the scroll object. The implementation of those operators is to execute `next()` or `previous()` and then replace the object with the result. The result of `next()` and `previous()` in the builder, however, is a Boolean value, so the scroll object will be lost.

Querying via the Hibernate Query Language (HQL)

Although the Hibernate Criteria Builder provides a way to express complicated queries, some people prefer a more SQL-like approach. The problem with exposing or working with SQL directly is that it violates the Don't Repeat Yourself (DRY) principle. With SQL, the logical mapping of fields onto their domain classes (already defined within the domain class itself) has to be repeated in the SQL. Hibernate provides an alternative query language for the database, called HQL. Using the SQL-like HQL syntax, the user can query Hibernate domain classes on the database in a more succinct and DRY approach.

The Basics of HQL and executeQuery

The key hook from GORM into HQL is the `executeQuery` method. This static method is attached to every GORM class and executes an arbitrary HQL query against the database. The particular class `executeQuery` is called on does not matter; the types of the objects returned is specified by the HQL itself.

The HQL language itself is very similar to SQL. Like SQL, it has three fundamental clauses: `select`, `from`, and `where`. In its most common basic usage, HQL uses a `from` clause to specify which domain class is being queried, and the `where` clause to specify constraints on the domain classes retrieved. The result of `executeQuery` is always a list of results.

Unlike SQL, only the `from` class is required. If the `where` clause is left off, all instances of that class are returned. If the `select` clause is left off, objects of the type specified immediately after `from` are returned. For more on using `select`, see "Retrieving Only Particular Fields with Projections" and "Retrieving Maps, Lists, and Objects Inline from HQL" later in this chapter.

Code Listing 3-26. HQL Basics

```
// In ./grails-app/domain/Foo.groovy
class Foo {
  int code1 = 0, code2 = 0
  static mapping = {
    table 'my_app_key_foo_t'
    code1 column:'code_prefix'
    code2 column:'code_suffix'
  }
}
// In ./test/integration/FooTests.groovy
void testHqlBasics() {
  [[1,2],[1,3],[4,4],[6,5]].each {
    assertNotNull new Foo(code1:it[0],

        code2:it[1]).save(flush:true)
  }
  assertEquals Foo.list(), Foo.executeQuery("from Foo")
  assertEquals Foo.findAllByCode1(1),
    Foo.executeQuery("from Foo where code1 = 1")
  assertEquals 2, Foo.executeQuery("""
    from Foo where code1 < code2
  """).size()
  assertTrue Foo.executeQuery("""
    from Foo where code1 < code2
  """).every { it.code1 < it.code2 }
```

```
assertTrue Foo.executeQuery("""
  from Foo where code1 = code2 and code1 = ?
""", [4]).every {
  it.code1 == 4; it.code1 == it.code2
}
}
```

Fully-Qualified Classes

HQL requires class names to be fully qualified. The easiest way to do this is through the idiom `$ClassName.name`. There is no great magic here—it is simply a call to the `getName()` method on the `ClassName` class object, which returns a fully-qualified class name as a String. That is then interpolated into the query.

Code Listing 3-27. Demonstrating Packaged Class HQL Idiom

```
// In ./grails-
app/domain/com/smokejumperit/eg/Baz.groovy
package com.smokejumperit.eg
class Baz { String value1 }
// In ./test/integration/BazTests.groovy
import com.smokejumperit.eg.Baz
class BazTests extends GroovyTestCase {
  void testHqlOnPackage() {
    assertNotNull new Baz(value1:'baz'
      ).save(flush:true)
    assertEquals 1,
      Baz.executeQuery("from $Baz.name").size()
  }
}
```

Retrieving Only Particular Fields with Projections

One of the primary advantages of HQL over the `findBy*` methods is the ability to select only the value of the fields from the domain object. This can provide a substantial improvement in performance when only a limited subset of information is needed from a domain class: the additional fields will not be fetched from the database and the object marshaling is bypassed altogether.

This functionality is called **querying projections**, and is implemented by using the `select` clause in a syntax very similar to SQL. If a single property is selected, the result will be a single-dimensional list of that property's values. If multiple properties are selected, the result will be a list of arrays of those properties' values.

Caution   It bears repeating that when multiple properties are selected, the values of the returned list are arrays, not lists. This is one of the author's largest annoyances with GORM. To get lists, `executeQuery` can be called as `executeQuery(query).collect { it as List }`. For another solution, see "Retrieving Maps, Lists, and Objects Inline from HQL".

Code Listing 3-28. Querying Projections via HQL

```
// In ./grails-app/domain/Foo.groovy
class Foo { int code1 = 0, code2 = 0 }
// In ./test/integration/FooTests.groovy
void testHqlProjections() {
  [[1,2],[1,3],[4,4],[6,5]].each {
    assertNotNull new Foo(code1:it[0],
                          code2:it[1]).save(flush:true)
  }
  assertEquals([1,1,4,6], Foo.executeQuery("""
```

```
      select code1 from Foo
  """))
  assertEquals([1,4,6], Foo.executeQuery("""
    select distinct code1 from Foo
  """))
  assertEquals([[1,2],[1,3],[4,4],[6,5]],
    Foo.executeQuery("""
      select code1,code2 from Foo
    """))
  }
```

Associations and Joins in HQL

One of the key differences between HQL and SQL is that HQL provides a natural way to navigate associations. Just as in Groovy, in HQL one-to-one and one-to-many associations can be navigated through dot notation. The class of the association does not even need to be specified in the `from` clause. For many-to-one or many-to-many associations an explicit join is needed.

Unlike in SQL, the join is specified by providing the navigation to those elements (see the examples that follow). As in SQL, joins may be `inner` (an end on the association is required), `left` (no parent end on the association is required), or `right` (no parent end of the association is required).

Note   When the `select` clause is not specified, all the domain objects specified in the `from` clause will be retrieved. This means that `from Foo f join f.bars b` will result in retrieving all the `[f,b]` pairings that exist in the database. To get around this, explicitly specify `select f`.

```
// In ./grails-app/domain/Foo.groovy
class Foo {
  static hasMany = [bars:Bar]
  Baz baz
}
// In ./grails-app/domain/Bar.groovy
class Bar {
  static belongsTo = [foo:Foo]
  String value
}
// In ./grails-app/domain/Baz.groovy
class Baz {
  static belongsTo = [foo:Foo]
  String value
}
// In ./test/integration/FooTests.groovy
void testJoin() {
  def foo = new Foo()
  foo.baz = new Baz(value:'baz')
  foo.addToBars(new Bar(value:'bar1'))
  foo.addToBars(new Bar(value:'bar2'))
  foo.addToBars(new Bar(value:'bar3'))
  assertNotNull foo.save()
  assertEquals(['baz'], Foo.executeQuery("""
    select f.baz.value from Foo f
  """))
  assertEquals([foo], Foo.executeQuery("""
    from Foo f where f.baz.value = 'baz'
  """))
```

```
  assertEquals(foo.bars*.id, Foo.executeQuery("""
    from Bar b where b.foo.baz.value = 'baz'
  """)*.id)
  assertEquals([foo], Foo.executeQuery("""
    select f from Foo f inner join f.bars b
    where b.value = 'bar1'
  """))
  assertEquals([foo, foo, foo],
    Foo.executeQuery("""
      select f from Foo f inner join f.bars b
      where b.value in
      ('bar1', 'bar2', 'bar3')
    """))
  assertEquals([['baz','bar1'],
               ['baz','bar2']],
    Foo.executeQuery("""
      select f.baz.value, b.value from Foo f
      join f.bars b
      where b.value in ('bar1','bar2')
    """).collect { it as List })
}
```

Retrieving Maps, Lists, and Objects Inline from HQL

An extremely useful but undoubtedly underappreciated and underutilized aspect of HQL is the ability to declare maps and objects inline. Within the `select` clause, HQL can construct maps and objects through use of the `new` keyword. The `new` keyword can be used in two ways: to invoke object constructors and to create maps and lists. In the case of object constructors, the selected properties are mapped directly into the constructor of the specified object before the results are returned. This provides a convenient shorthand for mapping database results into business objects.

It is important to note that the object need not be a Hibernate domain class; it simply needs to provide an appropriate constructor. In the case of maps and lists, the `new` keyword is followed by the word `map` or `list` (respectively), and creates a map or list of the selected properties.

Code Listing 3-30. Defining Maps, Lists, and Objects Directly in HQL

```groovy
// In ./grails-app/domain/Foo.groovy
class Foo { String value1, value2 }
// In ./src/groovy/Name.groovy
class Name {
  String first, last
  public Name(String firstName, String lastName) {
    first = firstName
    last = lastName
  }
  boolean equals(Name them) {
    return this.first == them?.first &&
           this.last == them?.last
  }
}
// In ./test/integration/FooTests.groovy
void testHqlConstructors() {
  assertNotNull new Foo(value1:'Robert',
                        value2:'Fischer').save()
  assertEquals([new Name('Robert', 'Fischer')],
    Foo.executeQuery("""
      select new Name(value1, value2) from Foo
    """))
  assertEquals([[foo:'Robert',bar:'Fischer']],
    Foo.executeQuery("""
      select new map(value1 as foo, value2 as bar)
```

```
        from Foo
    """))
assertEquals([['Robert', 'Fischer']],
    Foo.executeQuery("""
        select new list(value1, value2) from Foo
    """))
```

Chapter 4: GORM Usage in Grails

Constructing GORM Objects in the Controller

In Grails applications the parameters of a request will often directly reflect the properties on a GORM object. In this case the GORM object can be constructed by routing the parameters of an action directly onto the properties of the domain object. This is done by way of the map constructor: simply execute new MyDomainClass(params). When doing this, all of the base types are properly set except for Date. Embedded types and associations are not set, so they will also need to be hand-rolled. Associations are instantiated for free, however, which makes their initialization straightforward.

Code Listing 4-1. Demonstrating Normal Assignment Approaches

```
// In ./grails-app/domain/Foo.groovy
class Foo {
   static embedded = ['name']
   String string
   int integer
   float floater
   Date date
   Name name
   Bar bar
}
// In ./grails-app/domain/Bar.groovy
class Bar {
   static belongsTo = [foo:Foo]
   String value
}
// In ./src/groovy/Name.groovy
```

```groovy
class Name {
  String first, last

  boolean equals(Name them) {
    return this.first == them?.first &&
           this.last == them?.last
  }
}
void testMapConstructor() {
  def map = [
    string:'foo',
    integer:'3',
    floater:'3.14159',
    date:new Date().toString(),
    name:[first:'Robert',
          last:'Fischer'],
    bar:[value:'bar']
  ]
  def foo = new Foo(map)
  assertEquals map.string, foo.string
  assertEquals map.integer,
               foo.integer?.toString()
  assertEquals map.floater,
               foo.floater?.toString()
  assertNotNull foo.bar
  assertNull foo.bar.value
  assertNull foo.name
  assertNull foo.date
}
void testPropertiesSetting() {
  def map = [
```

```
      string:'foo',
      integer:'3',
      floater:'3.14159',
      date:new Date().toString(),
      name:[first:'Robert',
            last:'Fischer'],
      bar:[value:'bar']
   ]
   def foo = new Foo()
   foo.properties = map
   assertEquals map.string, foo.string
   assertEquals map.integer,
                foo.integer?.toString()
   assertEquals map.floater,
                foo.floater?.toString()
   assertNotNull foo.bar
   assertNull foo.bar.value
   assertNull foo.name
   assertNull foo.date
 }
```

Tip   There is a very handy method in the Apache Commons Lang
project, specifically in the `org.apache.commons.lang.time.DateUtils`
class: `parseDate(String,String[])`. This class will parse a given date
string against an entire series of possible candidate formats.

However, there is a significant security concern when using a controller's
parameters as input for the map constructor. Because parameters are
provided by the user and easily set for any arbitrary value, it is very
possible for the user to set a property that should only be set by the system.

This is handled by the `bindData` method of the controller, which can be called to exclude or include certain parameters. For more information on this method, see the Grails documentation at `http://grails.org/doc/1.1.x/` (Section 6.1.6).

Applications often use `bindData` in multiple different locations—the data to construct new instances may come in from many different places. Duplicating what properties to assign in many different places can be problematic, so it's often best to define the list of ineligible properties as a static property right on the class. Using this approach, all the calls to `bindData` will look like this: `bindData(target, params, excludes: Target.excludeProperties)`. Wrapping this logic in a helper method can make things even cleaner.

Working with Error Messages

Because Grails builds in internationalization, presenting errors in Grails is a bit trickier than in other frameworks—the translation from programmatic error state to human-readable message is somewhat involved. In other frameworks the ORM system is frequently responsible for presenting errors. This becomes a major difficulty when internationalizing the application. Similar to how views decouple presentation from the controllers, the i18n capabilities of GORM decouple presentation away from the GORM framework itself.

In a view, the key tags for message presentation are `g:hasErrors`, `g:eachError`, and `g:message`. These three respectively provide the ability to check for errors, iterate over the errors, and present the messages for the errors. There is another even more magical tag called `g:renderErrors`, which renders the errors directly as a list. However, the lack of configurability of the resulting HTML can be an issue with this tag.

Code Listing 4-2. Demonstrating Error Rendering in Views

```
// In ./grails-app/domain/Foo.groovy
class Foo { String string }
// In ./grails-app/controllers/EgController.groovy
class EgController {
  def errorMessage = {
    def foo = new Foo()
    foo.validate()
    [foo:foo]
  }
}
// In ./grails-app/views/eg/errorMessage.gsp
<html><head></head><body>
  <g:hasErrors bean="${foo}">
    <ul>
      <g:eachError bean="${foo}">
        <li><g:message error="${it}"/></li>
      </g:eachError>
    </ul>
  </g:hasErrors>
  <!-- More magical approach -->
  <g:hasErrors bean="${foo}">
    <g:renderErrors bean="${foo}" />
  </g:hasErrors>
</body></html>
```

Outside of the context of a view, the messageSource bean from the Spring application context can be used to get error messages. The messageSource bean is an instance of the Spring framework's org.springframework.context.MessageSource interface. The errors property attached to each GORM class can be fed into the messageSource bean along with a `java.util.Locale` to get human-readable error messages.

Code Listing 4-3. Demonstrating Messages from `messageSource`

```
def foo = new Foo()
foo.validate(
foo.errors*.allErrors.flatten().each {
  assertNotNull(
messageSource.getMessage(it, Locale.default)
)
    }
```

Tip   Error messages generated by the default i18n settings are fairly technical but can be modified by altering the appropriate code in `./grails-app/i18n/messages*`. The particular code to be modified is specified in the constraint documentation (and is often easy to guess), and the particular file to be modified is either `messages.properties` (when no locale is set) or `messages`, whose name contains the language code.

Lazy Initialization and the Grails Session

It seems to be a deep temptation for web application developers to throw objects—and sometimes even entire data structures—into the user's session. This should be discouraged for many reasons, including performance, concurrency, and audit concerns. When GORM objects are attached to users' sessions, there is the additional concern of the Hibernate session underlying it.

When fetched from the database, GORM objects are attached to a Hibernate session, which provides the functionality to actually communicate with the database. When the GORM object is attached to a user session and that session is marshaled after the request, the Hibernate session is detached from the GORM object. This means that the GORM object is no longer able to communicate with the database, which means that calls to `save` will fail, along with lazily-initialized associations, lazily-initialized properties, and a significant additional amount of functionality. In short, these GORM objects require a Hibernate session to be functional, and drawing the object from the user session results in the object not having a Hibernate session.

The simplest solution is to use the Hibernate `SessionFactory` (provided as a Spring bean named `sessionFactory`) to reattach GORM objects from the user session to the Hibernate session. This is done by way of the `merge` method on Hibernate's `Session` class. A potential source of bugs when doing this is to assume that the merge modifies the state of the merged object. While this may be true, caching may result in a different instance being returned. Therefore it is very important to use the result of the `merge` call as the instance moving forward.

Code Listing 4-4. Demonstrating Reattaching an Object

```
def hibSession = sessionFactory.currentSession
def foo = new Foo(string:'string')
assertNotNull foo.save()
assertTrue hibSession.contains(foo)
hibSession.evict(foo)
assertFalse hibSession.contains(foo)
foo = hibSession.merge(foo) // MUST do assign here
assertTrue hibSession.contains(foo)
```

A more systematic approach is to create a filter that scans the session for domain classes in `afterView` and replaces them with an object that holds an ID and the class to create. A dynamically-generated HQL query can then be used to reconstitute the object in `before`. When doing this, unpersisted changes are lost,[9] but substantially less content must be stored in the user's session and the object will be properly attached to the Hibernate session.

Lazy Initialization and Open Session in View

The Scenario: Accessing GORM from the View

The theory behind MVC design dictates that model objects should be loaded and managed by the controller, and the view should simply consume simple, raw pieces of data for presentation.

The reality, of course, is a bit more complicated. Often views—especially layouts and taglibs—will end up executing their own queries. Some views do not even have controllers backing them, yet need to draw information from the database.

When an instance is drawn from the database in a view, the Hibernate session is immediately closed. This is done to prevent accidental data updates from the view, since (according to theory) the view should not be talking to the model anyway. The downside of the Hibernate session being closed is that lazily-retrieved collections will throw a `org.hibernate.LazyInitializationException`, effectively forcing the query to aggressively fetch all the collections (and subcollections, and sub-subcollections) that may be needed downstream. Aside from being grossly inefficient, this is also not maintainable, because it basically requires exposing a deep view of internal structures at the point of the query. The situation only gets worse when multiple queries are involved.

---

[9] Of course, the filter's `after` closure could call `save` to address this issue.

The Solution: Open Session in View Filter

Grails provides an opt-in web application filter called
`GrailsOpenSessionInViewFilter`. This filter extends Spring's
`OpenSessionInViewFilter` and leaves the session open for the view.
Because the flush mode is set to `FlushMode.AUTO`, there is the potential for
the view to write to the database.

To implement this filter, execute `grails install-templates` to take
command of the `web.xml` directly. Edit the `web.xml` file in
`./src/templates/war/web.xml` and add the code shown in Code
Listing 4-5 near the other filters and filter mappings.

Code Listing 4-5. Installing the Open Session in View Filter

```
<!-- OSIV -->
<filter><!-- Declares the filter -->
  <filter-name>openSessionInViewFilter</filter-name>
  <filter-class>
org.codehaus.groovy.grails.orm.hibernate.support.GrailsO
penSessionInViewFilter
  </filter-class>
</filter>
<filter-mapping><!-- Installs the filter on all URLs -->
  <filter-name>openSessionInViewFilter</filter-name>
  <url-pattern>/*</url-pattern>
</filter-mapping>
<!-- /OSIV -->
```

Customizing and Tuning Grails Data Source Defaults

While Grails provides a solid default configuration for the application data
source (including pooling), in high-load circumstances with intense
database activity some additional tuning may be necessary.

Simple tuning of the Grails data source can be done by modifying values at runtime in `BootStrap.conf`. The `dataSource` Spring bean is an instance of `org.apache.commons.dbcp.BasicDataSource` and provides a wide range of configuration options.

More extensive configuration can be done by overriding the `dataSource` Spring bean completely. To do this, use the Spring Bean Builder DSL in the `./grails-app/conf/spring/resources.groovy` file. The bean needs to implement `javax.sql.DataSource`, but is otherwise fair game for configuration or modification.

Because the Hibernate properties are set only via `./grails-app/conf/DataSource.groovy`, that file is already kept in play. To prevent reduplication of effort, it is therefore best to use the data source information provided in the configuration. To accomplish this, import the Grails `ConfigurationHolder` and use the `config.dataSource` values `username`, `password`, `driverClassName`, and `url`.

Code Listing 4-6. Example Override of the `dataSource` Bean

```
// In ./grails-app/conf/spring/resources.groovy
import com.mchange.v2.c3p0.ComboPooledDataSource
import
org.codehaus.groovy.grails.commons.ConfigurationHolder
as CH
beans = {
    dataSource(ComboPooledDataSource) { bean ->
        bean.destroyMethod = 'close'
        user = CH.config.dataSource.username
        password = CH.config.dataSource.password
        driverClass = CH.config.dataSource.driverClassName
        jdbcUrl = CH.config.dataSource.url
        acquireIncrement = 5
        acquireRetryDelay = 10
```

```
    autoCommitOnClose = true
    automaticTestTable = 'c3p0_test'
}
```

Chapter 5: Filling in the Gaps with Groovy SQL and Spring's JDBC Support

Groovy SQL in Grails

The Role of Groovy SQL in Grails

Although the primary way of interacting with the database in Grails is GORM, and although HQL provides a mostly clean SQL replacement, more direct SQL work may occasionally be necessary. The most usual case for this is when an alternative data source, legacy table, or database-specific call is needed for only a couple situations: more systematic solutions would be overkill in that case. Another possible use is for optimizing calls: if a high-performance database trick (such as using a materialized view) is accessible but not being used by GORM or HQL, a domain class could provide a special-case query method to retrieve the appropriate IDs from the database and then fall back to `getAll` to retrieve the actual domain objects. These kinds of surgical persistence issues are where Groovy SQL can save the day in Grails.

Groovy SQL Basics

Groovy SQL is based directly on JDBC. It provides a collection of objects that wrap common JDBC actions and include simple hooks to existing calls. All of these capabilities are contained within the `groovy.sql` package, with the key class being `groovy.sql.Sql`. The methods of this class are simple: they take SQL as a String (or GString) and an optional list of positional parameter values, and either return the response or process the response with a provided closure. In any case, `Sql` takes care of managing all the JDBC objects. The particular method that is called specifies the nuances of behavior.

Table 5-1. Groovy SQL Methods

Method Name	Description	Variations
call	Used to execute stored procedures	String; String/Closure; String/List/Closure
eachRow	Used to process results row by row	String/Closure; String/List/Closure; String/Closure (MetaData)/Closure
execute	Simply executes SQL	String; String/List
executeInsert	Executes insert and returns auto-generated columns (`ids`)	String; String/List
executeUpdate	Executes update and returns a count of affected rows	String; String/List
firstRow	Executes a query and returns only the first row	String; String/List
query	Executes a query and hands the ResultSet to closure to process	String/Closure; String/List/Closure
rows	Executes a query and returns the rows of the result set as a List	String; String/Closure (MetaData); String/List

Additionally, the following methods provide configuration of the JDBC objects used by the `Sql` object:

- `setResultSetConcurrency(int)` sets the result set to read only (`ResultSet.CONCUR_READ_ONLY`) or updatable (`ResultSet.CONCUR_UPDATE`).

- `setResultSetHoldability(int)` indicates whether to leave cursors open at commit (`ResultSet.HOLD_CURSORS_OVER_COMMIT`) or close at commit (`ResultSet.CLOSE_CURSORS_AT_COMMIT`).

- `setResultSetType(int)` signifies the scrolling sensitivity of the result set: forward only (`ResultSet.TYPE_FORWARD_ONLY`), scrollable but does not reflect changes made by others (`ResultSet.TYPE_SCROLL_INSENSITIVE`), or scrollable and reflecting changes made by others (`ResultSet.TYPE_SCROLL_SENSITIVE`).

- `withStatement(Closure)` performs arbitrary configuration on the `Statement` objects used by this `Sql` instance. Each time a new `Statement` is created it is fed into the closure so the user might be corrected.

Injecting Groovy `Sql` Objects via Spring

In Grails, the data source is managed as a Spring bean named `dataSource`. This means that Spring's dependency injection is going to be the easiest way to configure a stand-alone `Sql` object that uses that `dataSource`. Two approaches can be used get such an object: the `dataSource` bean can be retrieved from Spring and hand-inserted into the `Sql` object, or the `Sql` object can be configured via Spring and accessed through its dependency injection.

Manually Instantiating the Sql Object

This approach is far and away the simplest. To manually instantiate the Sql object, simply get the dataSource bean though its dependency injection and call the constructor.

Code Listing 5-1. Demonstrating Manual Instantiation of Sql

```
// In ./test/integration/GsqlTests.groovy
import groovy.sql.Sql
class GsqlTests extends GroovyTestCase {
  def dataSource // Dependency-injected dataSource
  void testInstantiateSqlObject() {
    def sql = new Sql(dataSource)
  }
}
```

Getting a Sql Object via Dependency Injection

To have Spring instantiate and inject the Sql object, define the Sql bean in ./grails-app/conf/spring/resources.groovy via the Spring Bean Builder syntax. There are a few catches which are important to note at this point. The first is that the Sql bean is not designed as a singleton, so a new instance is required each time the Sql bean is injected. To accomplish this set the scope to 'prototype'. The second is that the dataSource bean is not local to the resources.groovy file and needs to be passed as a constructor call, so the syntax for injecting it is a bit odd (see Code Listing 5-2).

Code Listing 5-2. Defining and Demonstrating a Sql Spring bean

```
// In ./grails-app/conf/spring/resources.groovy
beans = {
    sql(groovy.sql.Sql,ref('dataSource')) { bean ->
      bean.scope = 'prototype'
    }
}
// In ./test/integration/GsqlTests.groovy
import groovy.sql.Sql
class GsqlTests extends GroovyTestCase {
  def sql // Dependency-injected groovy.sql.Sql
  void testSqlInjected() {
    assertNotNull("Is null", sql)
    assertEquals("Is wrong class", Sql, sql.class)
  }
}
```

Using Groovy Sql Objects with GORM Transactions

When intermingling GORM and Groovy SQL, always make sure the `Sql` object is placed within the same transaction; otherwise, a rollback on GORM may not impact the Groovy SQL. To link the two together, the `Sql` construct the object based on the same connection as the GORM object itself. Take care when working with this connection, because GORM's underlying Spring/Hibernate structures are doing their own tracking of the connection state. Therefore, things like transaction management should not be handled directly through the `Sql` object.

To get access to the GORM connection, inject the `sessionFactory` bean and then use the connection provided by `sessionFactory`. `currentSession.connection()` to construct the `Sql` object. The SQL executed against that object will be in the same JDBC connection context as GORM.

Code Listing 5-3. Constructing a GORM-Connected Sql Object

```
// In ./test/integration/GsqlTests.groovy
import groovy.sql.Sql
class GsqlTests extends GroovyTestCase {
  def sessionFactory
  void testGormConnectedSession() {
    def sql = new Sql(
      sessionFactory.currentSession.connection()
    )
  }
}
```

Spring's JDBC Support in Grails

The Role of Spring JDBC Support in Grails

Although Spring's JDBC Support is no doubt the best pure Java library for interacting with JDBC, its position in Grails is mostly architectural. In Grails, GORM, services and Groovy SQL accomplish those tasks that Spring JDBC Support is normally used for. In many cases the dynamic nature of Groovy and its closure supports make the capabilities of Spring JDBC redundant. However, because Grails is so tightly coupled with Java and leverages so many Java libraries, Spring JDBC Support is sometimes still needed as a way to interact with those libraries.

Using Groovy to Concisely Implement Spring JDBC Support

The basis of Spring JDBC Support is a series of monad-like interfaces. The interfaces, such as `PreparedStatementCreator` and `ResultSetExtractor`, implement a single method and are used similarly to Groovy's closures. This structure is easy to implement inline by using the magic as operator: it can convert a closure directly into an implementation of a single-method interface. This makes using Spring JDBC Support much easier and replaces the anonymous inner class idiom in Java.

Code Listing 5-4. Using Groovy's as operator to Define JDBC Support Implementations

```
// In ./test/integration/SpringJdbcTests.groovy
import org.springframework.jdbc.core.*
import java.sql.*
class SpringJdbcTests extends GroovyTestCase {
 def dataSource
  void testCoercionToJdbcTypes() {
    def jdbc = new JdbcTemplate(dataSource)
    def prepStater = { Connection conn ->
      conn.prepareStatement("SELECT 1 FROM foo")
    } as PreparedStatementCreator
    def rsHandler = { ResultSet rs ->
      return "foobar"
    } as ResultSetExtractor
    assertEquals("foobar",
      jdbc.query(prepStater, rsHandler)
    )
  }
}
```

Injecting Spring JDBC Support Beans

Not surprisingly, Spring JDBC Support beans are designed to work very well with Spring dependency injection. To add Spring JDBC Support beans to the Spring context, define the beans in ./grails-app/conf/spring/

resources.groovy. The bean will probably require a Data Source passed in the constructor, and because the dataSource bean is not local to that file, it will need to be acquired via the Spring DSL ref method.

Code Listing 5-5. Example of Defining a JDBC Support Bean

```
// In ./grails-app/conf/spring/resources.groovy
import org.springframework.jdbc.core.*
beans = {
    jdbcTemplate(JdbcTemplate,ref('dataSource'))
}
```

Copyright

Grails Persistence with GORM and GSQL

© 2009 by Robert Fischer

ISBN-13 (electronic): 978-1-4302-1927-9

ISBN-13 (paperback): 978-1-4302-1926-2

Distributed to the book trade in the United States by Springer-Verlag New York, Inc., 233 Spring Street, 6th Floor, New York, NY 10013, and outside the United States by Springer-Verlag GmbH & Co. KG, Tiergartenstr. 17, 69112 Heidelberg, Germany.

In the United States: phone 1-800-SPRINGER, fax 201-348-4505, e-mail orders@springer-ny.com, or visit http://www.springer-ny.com. Outside the United States: fax +49 6221 345229, e-mail orders@springer.de, or visit http://www.springer.de.

For information on translations, please contact Apress directly at 2855 Telegraph Ave, Suite 600, Berkeley, CA 94705. Phone 510-549-5930, fax 510-549-5939, e-mail info@apress.com, or visit http://www.apress.com.

Printed in the United States
146975LV00004B/2/P